D0822888

A UNITED NATIONS EMERGENCY PEACE SERVICE

TO PREVENT GENOCIDE AND CRIMES AGAINST HUMANITY

Robert C. Johansen, Editor

Published with the support of:

Global Action to Prevent War
Nuclear Age Peace Foundation
World Federalist Movement

© 2006 by Global Action to Prevent War, Nuclear Age Peace Foundation, and World Federalist Movement

All rights reserved.

No part of this publication may be reproduced, stored in a retrieval system, or transmitted in any form, or by any means, electronic, mechanical, photocopying, recording, or otherwise, without the written permission of the publisher.

Cover Design: Casey Lynn
Interior Design: Scott Barrie and Sarah Van Male, Cyanotype Book Architects

Published by World Federalist Movement - Institute for Global Policy, 708 Third Avenue, 24th Floor, New York, NY 10017, USA.

Printed in the United States of America by BRIOprint.

ISBN 0-9710727-6-0
LCCN 2006927109

CONTENTS

ACKNOWLEDGEMENTS

We thank the many individuals who have steadfastly worked to promote an initiative that, when realized, will prevent genocide and crimes against humanity. When this book's proposal for a United Nations Emergency Peace Service eventually bears fruit, these individuals, and those readers who decide to join hands with them, will finally deliver on the often-voiced promise, "Never again!" We want to thank the donors, members, and staffs of Global Action to Prevent War, the Nuclear Age Peace Foundation, and the World Federalist Movement, whose support has been absolutely essential. For their leadership in public affairs and their analysis and commentary in this book, we thank Lois Barber, Lt. Gen. Satish Nambiar, Hussein Solomon, and Alcides Costa Vaz. We are inspired by and deeply appreciate the enduring commitment of Sir Brian Urquhart to the prevention of genocide and the creation of a more peaceful world.

For their vital programmatic work and intellectual contributions we also thank all those who participated in the Santa Barbara and Cuenca meetings, and in numerous conference calls, in order to build a realistic proposal with broad consensus. We have listed these persons in the Appendix. The present proposal is a product of a deliberative process, both intellectual and political, in which the views of all participants have shaped the proposal. We especially thank H. Peter Langille for his scholarship over many years on all matters related to this proposal, for his early drafts presented at the Santa Barbara meetings, and for his subsequent contributions at every point along the way.

We also thank those who graciously donated their time and expertise to this project: Casey Lynn for her cover design; Scott Barrie and Sarah Van Male of Cyanotype Book Architects for their layout work; Robert Zuber for help in editing; William Reynolds and BRIOprint for printing; and the Rutgers Law School (Newark) for their logistical support. We thank Waverly de Bruijn for her patient, thoughtful, expert coordination of all aspects of this project, for her persistently good-natured attitude toward all participants, and for her commitment to the substantive goals of this project. For earlier and similarly expert help and commitment, we thank Jennifer Nordstrom.

We also thank the Ford Foundation, whose generous support made this publication possible, and the Simons Foundation for its vital, general support of the project to create a United Nations Emergency Peace Service.

David Krieger, Nuclear Age Peace Foundation
Saul Mendlovitz, Global Action to Prevent War
William Pace, World Federalist Movement
Robert C. Johansen, Editor

PREFACE

Sir Brian Urquhart

In 1948, the first Secretary-General of the United Nations, Trygve Lie, proposed during a commencement speech at Harvard the development of a small, dedicated UN force to deal with the violent and chaotic conditions in Jerusalem. Perhaps unwisely, he called it a "United Nations Legion." In any case, the proposal was greeted with thunderous silence from the permanent members of the Security Council; even the United States and the USSR agreed that it was a terrible idea. The violence in Jerusalem continued.

UN peacekeeping came into full bloom with the 1956 Suez crisis and the creation of the first UN Emergency Force (UNEF I). That force was deployed, due to the leadership and determination of Dag Hammarskjold and Ralph Bunche, within eight days of the General Assembly's decision to establish it. The early peacekeeping forces of the Cold War period were put into the field with similar speed, the record being seventeen hours for UNEF II (to preserve a cease-fire between Egypt and Israel) in 1973. Although the political stakes were often very high, those early forces were less complex than the post-Cold-War multifunctional operations that were later deployed within the frontiers of a single disturbed country. Except for the 1960 Congo operation, these early forces had little or no humanitarian responsibilities. Equally important, they dealt only with governments and national forces and were deployed with the agreement of those governments as soon as a cease-fire was in place.

Although in the early days of its existence a standing rapid deployment force was accepted without major criticism from states parties, such a force became really indispensable when, in the 1990s, the Security Council agreed to set up seventeen multifunctional peacekeeping/humanitarian missions in quick succession. The role of these operations was far more complex than the original peacekeeping operations, and the humanitarian crises facing most of them meant that even a month or two of delay in deployment was devastating not only for the victims, but also to the mission's effectiveness and subsequent authority. Moreover, very few of their contingents were trained in the fundamental tasks of stopping random violence and dealing with chaos and disorder. This was why situations like that in Sierra Leone, where the rebel faction more or less successfully immobilized a UN force, could easily develop.

The failure to deploy forces in emergency situations can start a chain reaction of disaster, loss of life, and misery. However, late deployment of a mission with forces untrained for the tasks at hand can create an equally devastating humanitarian situation. In her recent, remarkable book, *The Turbulent Decade,* Sadako Ogata, the High Commissioner for Refugees in the 1990s, describes vividly what the absence of trained forces can mean for a large refugee population in whose camps there is no one to keep order or stop factional abuse. The post-Rwandan-genocide refugee crisis in the Great Lakes Region led to homicidal chaos that has so far cost over four million lives as well as many millions of dollars in relief aid and general economic loss. Tragedy in the camps continues despite the eventual arrival of a UN peacekeeping force. Much of this might have been avoided if, in the early stages, Ogata's pleas for immediate military assistance had not been ignored.

I have mentioned this one example because it helps address some of the most common objections to a standing rapid deployment force or, as it is called in this book, an Emergency Peace Service. There are several common objections to this idea, as well as one seldom expressed but very important. The first common objection is related to *expense.* Certainly even a small standing force would be quite expensive by United Nations standards, though it would still be exponentially less costly than prolonged disasters like the continuing tragedy in the Great Lakes region—in lives, in economic and social disruption and in the cost of humanitarian and other assistance year after year, including at present a UN peacekeeping force that shows no sign of leaving any time soon.

Another popular argument against a standing emergency service is grounded in a belief that "standby arrangements" with governments can and should be enlisted to handle these tasks. That, unfortunately, is not always true. In 1994, there were more than twenty standby arrangements with governments for the provision of peacekeeping forces. *Not one could be activated successfully when the Security Council belatedly decided that something ought to be done about the Rwandan genocide.* Later on, when Sadako Ogata appealed for help in controlling the very large refugee camps set up outside the borders of Rwanda, only one standby agreement could be activated, and that for so short a time that Ogata ended up asking president Mobutu of Zaire, who was about to be overthrown, for assistance from the Zairean army. Any government has a perfect right *not* to send its troops into disagreeable and dangerous situations, which is more often than not what the UN has to deal with. Only a professional, specially trained, standing UN force at the full disposal of the Security Council can be absolutely relied on to respond with the necessary speed in such situations. At present, this does not exist. As Kofi Annan once said, the UN is the only fire brigade in the world that has to acquire a fire engine after the fire has started.

However, the most basic objection to a standing UN peace service is seldom expressed publicly. Protection of national sovereignty is a concern that very often limits the ability of the UN to do the right thing in the right way at the right time. Fear of any UN development that may erode national sovereignty has always limited the UN's capacity for intervention. For this same reason, governments have been acutely cautious about expanding the Secretary-General's sphere of authority. A standing emergency peace service would certainly increase the Security Council's capacity to react quickly and effectively in an emergency, rather than go through the pedestrian and often untimely and unsatisfactory process of setting up a traditional peace-keeping force. Nevertheless, it seems as though it will take more disasters and many more debates before the governments that object to a standing UN rapid deployment force can be convinced that saving lives and stopping incipient disasters before they run out of control is more important, and far less dangerous, than any possible threat to national sovereignty.

Meanwhile, it is vitally necessary that the concept and the practical plan for making an emergency peace service a reality be kept alive. That is the crucial importance of this book.* The basic proposal begins by stating, "Because governments have not created the necessary UN capability, the responsibility for breathing life into the UN Emergency Peace Service now lies with civil society, working with allies in the UN and interested governments." This venture is of the greatest importance both to the UN as a responsible institution and to the millions as of yet unknown, innocent victims who might, in the future, be saved by this essential addition to the UN's capacity to act on their behalf. Like many visionary ideas, there are several plausible objections to a UN Emergency Peace Service, or whatever it might finally be called. Nevertheless, there is one overwhelming argument *for* it. It is desperately needed, and it is needed as soon as possible.

*As one who has been associated with the idea of a standing United Nations emergency force or service since the earliest years of the world organization, I would like to congratulate all those who have made this book possible—Saul Mendlovitz, Bill Pace, David Krieger, the Editor Robert C. Johansen and all their associates. I should also like to mention Peter Langille, who has worked tirelessly with this subject for many years and has authored many of the documents and policy papers that provide a very useful context for this proposal.

INTRODUCTION

David Krieger, Saul Mendlovitz, William Pace

Today's Reality

Tragically, violent outbreaks continue to plague human civilization, in which innocent people are ruthlessly killed simply because of their national, ethnic, racial, or religious identities. It is now widely recognized, however, that such mass killings and other crimes against humanity are clearly prohibited in international law. In addition, leading experts and numerous international commissions affirm that the international community could prevent many of these crimes *if* it would quickly send a professional security force to enforce the law in humanitarian crises, such as should have happened in Rwanda in 1994. Yet, the international community lacks the necessary capability to deploy such a law-enforcing body promptly where innocent people face threats to their dignity, their homes, and their lives.

In recent years, concerned governments, several United Nations study groups such as the High-level Panel on Threats, Challenges and Change, and statements by the UN Secretary-General and by independent experts have all stressed the need for a more effective rapid-reaction capability to stop such crimes whenever possible. The need is clear. Yet, unless concerned citizens and officials throughout the world commit themselves to a set of principles and a desirable model of enforcement, an effective force to prevent such crimes will not be established. We will find ourselves again and again saying "never again." The time has come to honor this bold commitment with solid action.

Toward this end, we have brought together a diverse coalition of individuals and organizations to form a Working Group for a United Nations Emergency Peace Service. We want to nurture a worldwide effort to reach out and bring within humanity's grasp a new instrument to help protect the innocent. Anyone with good intentions and a concern for preventing the most egregious international criminal acts can hardly be against the idea that undergirds the proposal in this book. The question is whether enough people with good intentions will act to implement it.

The world has lived with genocide and crimes against humanity for far too long. Awareness of the need to prevent these crimes has grown from the tragic experience of the holocaust of World War II and other cases of genocide and crimes against humanity that preceded and have occurred since this war. Following World War II, the leaders of the defeated Axis nations were held to account in the Nuremberg and Tokyo war crimes tribunals for crimes against the peace, war crimes, and crimes against humanity. The widely endorsed Nuremberg Charter made clear that all persons are subject to international law, regardless of the laws of their state, and that no person, even heads of state and government, stands above international law. In 1948, the Convention on the Prevention and Punishment of the Crime of Genocide was opened for signatures in an attempt to prevent any further instances of this heinous crime. In 1998, 120 countries agreed to the Rome Statute of the International Criminal Court to create the world's first permanent International Criminal Court where individuals accused of genocide, crimes against humanity and war crimes could be held to account.

Although these accomplishments and subsequent UN efforts to improve its rapid reaction capability have been important measures, they have not been sufficient. To stop genocide and crimes against humanity, the next logical and essential step is the creation of a United Nations Emergency Peace Service (UNEPS), a small, highly mobile standing United Nations rapid deployment capability that could be the first responder to potential cases of genocide and crimes against humanity.

Readers should understand that the proposal contained in these pages is a work in progress. New ideas and participants, as well as a healthy sense of the global commonweal, will doubtless re-shape some of its contours. Moreover, other initiatives already underway in the United Nations and regional settings are absolutely necessary. UNEPS will not replace these. Rather they will enable UNEPS to do its work better. Similarly, UNEPS should also enable some of them to get off the ground more effectively. UNEPS is the missing instrument in a much larger tool box for building peace, strengthening security, and upholding human rights.

This volume makes the case that a UN Emergency Peace Service is needed and explains how it might be structured and function. Readers may gain a quick overview of the proposal by reading first the Executive Summary in Chapter 1.

Historical Context

Before more fully introducing the contents of this volume, it may be helpful to describe this initiative's roots in a much longer process of expanding human dignity and justice. Genocide is one of the key crimes that UNEPS is being designed to prevent. Although the international community has been slow in addressing this crime through the long sweep of history, significant progress has been made in our lifetimes. The term "genocide" did not even exist in any language until 1943. As he surveyed mass murder during Nazi occupation of Europe, Raphael Lemkin, a Polish Jewish legal scholar, linguist, and philosopher, first coined the word.[1] Genocide is a composite of two words, *genos* (Greek) meaning a designated class and in this instance, an identified human group, and *cide* (Latin) meaning killing. Genocide, then, is the killing of a human group.

Recognition that genocide is indeed a criminal act has gradually increased over many years. It was considered part of crimes against humanity in the Nuremberg Trials of high-ranking Nazi officials. Through the prodigious efforts of Lemkin and others, the UN General Assembly unanimously passed a resolution establishing the Convention on the Prevention and Punishment of the Crime of Genocide in 1948.

The treaty defines genocide as "acts committed with intent to destroy in whole or in part a national, ethnical, racial or religious group." As of this writing, 138 states have ratified the convention. Although Article VIII has not been used as a basis for UN action, it states that "any contracting party may call upon the competent organs of the United Nations to take such actions under the Charter . . . as they consider appropriate for the prevention and suppression of acts of genocide. . . ."

To assign to government officials as *individuals* a responsibility for honoring the law against genocide has brought a fundamental change in international law akin to a paradigm shift in the natural sciences. From the origins of international law in the 1600s until the time of Nuremberg, an axial principle of sovereignty had allowed national officials to engage in any murderous behavior they chose within their own territories, without review by external powers. States were strictly prohibited from interfering in the internal matters of other states, albeit when the behavior of national officials was deemed extremely egregious, political elites from other polities would occasionally lodge letters of protest. However, for centuries the notion that a state might intervene militarily to curtail acts of officials in another state was unthinkable. For example, in 1916 when U.S. Ambassador Henry Morgenthau protested the Turkish massacre of Armenians, the Turkish government denied the charges, and the U.S. Department of State, despite Morgenthau's urgings, even refused to lodge a formal protest. Yet today the law is that "persons committing genocide . . . shall be punished, whether they are constitutionally responsible rulers, public officials or private individuals."[2]

As already noted, the view of sovereignty that shielded officials from formal indictment and judicial process for acts undertaken within their own territories was maintained until Nuremberg. During the time of Napoleon to Kaiser Wilhelm, even officials who lost wars were either imprisoned or exiled rather than tried for possible criminal acts. The establishment of the two international *ad hoc* criminal tribunals to address gross violations of human rights in the former Yugoslavia and Rwanda in the 1990s and the establishment of the permanent International Criminal Court (ICC) in 2002 have further underscored the recognition that no one is allowed to commit genocide, crimes against humanity, or war crimes with impunity. Indeed, the statute of the ICC, which 100 countries have ratified, carries broad authority and specific jurisdiction to try individuals indicted for such crimes, clearly demonstrating the severity attached to them.[3] In addition, the concept of "responsible sovereignty" is becoming widely accepted, establishing the norm that if governments do not protect their own citizens from gross violations of their rights, then the rulers lose their sovereign immunity and the international community has a *duty* to intervene for the purpose of protecting victims against gross violations.

The Proposal in Context

A transnational coalition of civil society organizations within the Working Group are vigorously promoting the establishment of a standing UN rapid-response force (which we label a "service" in part because it is designed to enforce law, not to conduct more conventional kinds of military activity). This coalition has generated the materials in this volume. The impetus stems from the dismal failure of the international community to prevent the slaughter of innocent civilians in Cambodia, Rwanda, Bosnia, East Timor, Liberia, Somalia, Darfur, and elsewhere. Rather than mobilizing for rapid intervention, national governments, the United Nations, and regional organizations have not responded in a timely or sufficiently robust fashion to counteract what is now understood to be the criminal behavior of genocide and crimes against humanity.

The coalition promoting the establishment of UNEPS believes that the inability and unwillingness to deal with genocide and crimes against humanity arises, at least in important part, from the absence of an appropriate body with authorization to enforce these laws. This remains true despite some efforts over the past three decades to address the inadequacy of UN peace operations, not only for preventing genocide and crimes against humanity but also for addressing interstate and intrastate armed conflict. For example, some 83 member states have registered to support the UN Standby Arrangement System (UNSAS), initiated in 1997.[4] In addition, 7 states organized what has become the multi-national Standby High Readiness Brigade for United Nations Operations (SHIRBRIG), which has seen action in Sudan.[5] Other coalitions, under the umbrella of formal organizations such as the African Union, are being formed in various regions of the world. Despite these initiatives, they do not provide a dedicated force prepared for immediate deployment, participating states often have reservations about deploying them, and some non-participating states remain skeptical about their formation. As Brian Urquhart notes in his preface to this volume, these arrangements are not sufficiently reliable to handle the preventive missions envisioned for UNEPS.

Industrial societies, which have material and personnel capacity to contribute to peace operations, are frequently inhibited from doing so by what is labeled the "body-bag backlash"—the concern that if military personnel are killed during humanitarian interventions, the public will question or even condemn the exercise as being insufficiently important to national interests. On the other hand, objections to an emergency force from countries in the Global South stem from a fear that deployments would occur in their regions without appropriate levels of participation, guidance and oversight from generally weaker states. Questions about organization, command and control, location of personnel, and financial support have also been raised. Obviously, confidence-building measures regarding political, structural, and financial matters must be addressed if there is to be an efficient, rapid response that is capable of dealing successfully with threats of genocide and crimes against humanity. We believe that the proposal for UNEPS, and the accompanying materials presented here, provide satisfactory answers to many of these challenges.

The Challenge

The transnational Working Group for a UN Emergency Peace Service has moved to this point with the help of many individuals and groups. Three organizations in particular, aided by their donors and foundation support, have nurtured this undertaking since it began in 2002. Global Action to Prevent War, under the auspices of the World Order Models Project, invited scholars and representatives from numerous civil society organizations interested in human rights or associated with the UN to preliminary discussions. These included Human Rights Watch, the World Federalist Movement, the Women's International League for Peace and Freedom, the United Nations Association of the United States of America, and a number of religious groups. The Nuclear Age Peace Foundation became involved in this project at a very early date as well. In 2003, the Foundation, along with the Simons Centre for Peace and Disarmament Studies at the Liu Institute for Global Issues, University of British Columbia, organized and hosted a UNEPS Symposium in Santa Barbara.[6] Symposium participants included diplomatic and security experts, academics, and social activists (see the Appendix for a list of participants). The World Federalist Movement (WFM) convened the working group meetings with Global Action to Prevent War preceding the Santa Barbara conference, and its Executive Director chaired the meetings leading to the seminal principles for the UNEPS proposal. WFM's Institute for Global Policy is the publisher of this book. As of this writing, the World Federal Movement, Global Action to Prevent War, and the Nuclear Age Peace Foundation serve as co-secretariats for the global UNEPS project and campaign.

Professor Robert C. Johansen of the Kroc Institute for International Peace Studies and political science professor at the University of Notre Dame served as rapporteur for the Working Group following the Santa Barbara meetings. Drawing upon the contributions of all participants, Johansen wrote the Executive Summary of the UNEPS proposal, which grew out of the Santa Barbara meetings and subsequent conference calls, as well as the longer rationale, "A United Nations Emergency Peace Service: To Prevent Genocide and Crimes Against Humanity" (chapter 2). This statement provides further detail on the proposal and has become the agreed-upon, central working paper for the Working Group. With some help from the Ford Foundation, experts gathered for intense discussions in a second workshop in Cuenca, Spain, in February 2005. Johansen again synthesized the results of this workshop in "Expert Discussion of the United Nations Emergency Peace Service: The Cuenca Report" (chapter 3). Of special interest in this chapter are the main principles on which participants agreed. These might form the nucleus around which additional support can build. His report also identifies important unresolved issues and questions for further research regarding the organization, authorization, use, and administration of the service. Johansen's preliminary report on the Cuenca workshop has been distributed electronically throughout the globe. It has proven very useful in engaging other individual and group partners.

Only a few brief words are needed to introduce the remainder of the materials in this volume. Brian Urquhart, who prepared the preface to this volume, is the former UN Under-Secretary-General for Special Political Affairs and a highly respected official who has worked on UN peace operations over many years with five different UN Secretaries-General. He is a leading voice for the establishment of a UN rapid response capability. Following the UNEPS documents prepared by Robert C. Johansen are several comments by other well-known experts. Lieutenant General Satish Nambiar of the Indian Armed Forces, and First Force Commander and Head of Mission of the United Nations forces in the former Yugoslavia from 1992-1993, comments on several dimensions of the Cuenca report. Questions being voiced by diverse constituencies throughout the world are discussed by Professor Hussein Solomon, Director of the Center for International Political Studies, University of Pretoria, South Africa; Professor Alcides Costa Vaz, the Director of the Institute of International Relations of the University of Brasilia, Brazil; and Lois Barber, Executive Director of EarthAction.

The Working Group is well aware that the issues raised by this proposal for a permanent UN Emergency Peace Service need to be widely discussed by members of the public, journalists, religious leaders, human rights organizations and others, as well as by governments, UN officials, and intergovernmental organizations throughout the world. We invite participation by all. Many in the UNEPS coalition participated in the effort to establish the International Criminal Court. We believe that the proposal for UNEPS is at a point similar to where the Court was in 1994, at a time when few were aware of the movement to create such a Court. Yet the Court came into being by 2002. With appropriate research, discussion, and coalition building, we believe the United Nations Emergency Peace Service can be established in the foreseeable future. Because this is a work in progress and one that we must not allow to fail, we welcome your comments and invite you to join this critically important global project to prevent future incidents of genocide and crimes against humanity.

Endnotes

[1] It first appeared in print in Lemkin's book *Axis Rule in Occupied Europe: Laws of Occupation, Analysis of Government, Proposals of Redress* (Washington: Carnegie Endowment for International Peace, 1944).

[2] Article IV of the United Nations Convention on the Prevention and Punishment of the Crime of Genocide.

[3] See the Rome Statute of the International Criminal Court, available at http://un-treaty.un.org/ENGLISH/bible/englishinternetbible/partI/chapterXVIII/treaty11.asp (last visited March 24, 2006).

[4] *See* "Member States in the UNSAS" dated April 15, 2005, available at http://www.un.org/Depts/dpko/milad/fgs2/unsas_files/status_report/statusreport15april05.pdf.pdf (last visited March 24, 2006).

[5] See "History of SHIRBRIG," available at http://www.shirbrig.dk/shirbrig/html/hist.htm (last visited March 24, 2006).

[6] The Simons Centre is now known as the Simons Centre for Disarmament and Non-Proliferation Research.

1

THE UNITED NATIONS EMERGENCY PEACE SERVICE
EXECUTIVE SUMMARY

Robert C. Johansen, Rapporteur

The Need

Despite the need at times to move quickly to prevent genocide, "ethnic cleansing," and crimes against humanity, the United Nations has no reliable capacity to move promptly, even if halting a catastrophe could save hundreds of thousands of lives. Genocide in Rwanda illustrates this incapacity, as do the massive killings of innocent people in Cambodia, the former Yugoslavia, East Timor, Sierra Leone, the Democratic Republic of the Congo, Liberia, the Sudan, and elsewhere.

The time has come to create a permanent UN Emergency Peace Service to ensure that the next preventable humanitarian disaster will not occur. If such a service had been established earlier, it could have prevented many of the atrocities that have killed millions of civilians, wounded millions more, forced tens of millions from their homes, destroyed entire economies, and wasted hundreds of billions of dollars. Of course such a service would not be a panacea for security problems in general; indeed it would be designed to complement—not replace—other essential national, regional, and United Nations efforts. Yet an Emergency Peace Service could provide immediate, full protection in some crises and serve as an advance group that would prepare the way for subsequent additional help, if needed, in larger conflicts—a vital function that is not provided by any existing agency. Such a service could also help address extreme environmental and natural disasters in cases where other remedies are inadequate for averting major threats to human life.

The Proposal

Because a UN Emergency Peace Service would be permanent, based at UN designated sites, and include mobile field headquarters, it could move to quell an emergency within 48 hours after United Nations authorization. Since it would be individually recruited from among volunteers from many countries, it would not suffer the reluctance of UN members to deploy their own national units. As its 12,000 to 15,000 personnel would be carefully selected, expertly trained, and coherently organized and commanded, it would not fail in its mission due to lack of skills, equipment, cohesiveness, experience in resolving conflicts, or gender, national, or religious imbalance. Because it would be an integrated service encompassing civilian, police, judicial, and military personnel prepared to conduct multiple functions in diverse UN operations, it would not suffer for lack of components essential to peace operations or from confusion about the chain of command. By providing a wide range of functions, the UN Emergency Peace Service would, for the first time in history, offer a rapid, comprehensive, internationally legitimate response to crisis.

The Plan of Action

Because governments have not created the necessary UN capability, the responsibility for breathing life into the United Nations Emergency Peace Service now lies with civil society, working with allies in the UN and interested governments. To create this service, a growing number of citizens' organizations and leaders of civil society are determined to: (1) identify interested parties throughout the world to expand the number and diversity of those committed to this initiative; (2) secure agreement on the principles, composition, and financing of a UN Emergency Peace Service; (3) draw on expert knowledge to ensure that the growing constituency is accurately informed and to write detailed plans for the Emergency Service and how to establish it; (4) develop a well-organized network of support with a compelling website, promotional materials, list of endorsements, and speakers' bureau; and (5) encourage a wide consultative process among non-governmental organizations, the UN system, and national governments to ensure the implementation of a successful strategy.

2

PROPOSAL FOR A UNITED NATIONS EMERGENCY PEACE SERVICE TO PREVENT GENOCIDE AND CRIMES AGAINST HUMANITY[1]

Robert C. Johansen, Rapporteur

The Need

Despite the need to be able to move quickly to prevent genocide and crimes against humanity, the United Nations has no capacity to avert such catastrophes, even when prompt action could save hundreds of thousands of lives. The international community's failure to stop genocide in Rwanda in 1994 and to avert "ethnic cleansing" occurring in the Darfur region of Sudan a decade later illustrate this incapacity, as do the other massive killings of civilians in Cambodia, the former Yugoslavia, East Timor, Sierra Leone, the Democratic Republic of the Congo, Liberia, and elsewhere. In recent years, huge atrocities have killed millions of innocent people, wounded millions more, forced tens of millions from their homes, destroyed entire economies, and wasted hundreds of billions of dollars.

After witnessing genocide, everyone promises: "Never again." But mass murder *has* happened again, and yet again. The time to stop it has come, at least in all those instances where the international community could have a reasonable probability of success. Yet existing international capabilities are simply unable to meet this responsibility. "Too little, too late" has become the rule rather than the exception. As the UN Secretary-General has warned, without serious reforms and institutional innovation, the United Nations will be unable to prevent future human catastrophes.[2] The conscience of every human being should be shocked and aroused by the international community's inability to quell atrocities in Darfur ten years after the lessons "learned" in Rwanda.[3]

Although many factors cause "too little, too late," a single innovation could address most of them: the creation of a permanent UN Emergency Peace Service to protect those victimized by war, genocide, and crimes against humanity. Such a service could save millions of lives and billions of dollars, while also advancing the rule of law against heinous crimes. Of course it would not be a panacea for security problems in general; indeed its purpose is to complement—not replace—other essential national, regional, and United Nations efforts. Yet such an Emergency Peace Service could provide immediate, full protection in some crises and serve as an advance group that would prepare the way for subsequent additional help when needed—a vital function that is not covered by any existing agency.[4] Such a service might also address environmental accidents and natural disasters where they threaten enormous loss of life and local and national governments are unable or unwilling to avert a severe humanitarian crisis.[5]

The time is finally right to create a permanent UN Emergency Peace Service to ensure that the next preventable humanitarian disaster will not occur. First, a growing number of people are acknowledging that every government's sovereign rights arise from an equally solemn responsibility to protect the people it governs. This duty, rooted in the concept of "sovereignty as responsibility," means a government is obligated to protect its people, to prevent crises that put its population at risk, to refuse to inflict arbitrary death on its citizens, and to bring equitable assistance to victimized people for recovery after a crisis.[6] "It is the peoples' sovereignty rather than the sovereign's sovereignty"[7] that is gaining weight in decision-making today. The state "is now widely understood to be the servant of its people, and not vice versa."[8] If a state clearly violates its sovereign responsibility, which includes accountability to its people, to its signature of the UN Charter, and to the entire international community of states responsible for compliance with human rights agreements, then the international community has a duty to stop massive death or other large-scale human suffering out of respect for peoples' sovereignty.[9] Indeed, ". . . the core challenge to the Security Council and to the United Nations as a whole in the next century," declared Secretary-General Annan, is "to forge unity behind the principle that massive and systematic violations of human rights—wherever they may take place—should not be allowed to stand." This is exactly what a UN Emergency Peace Service could do.

In addition, an impressive number of studies carried out by the United Nations, by national governments, and by independent experts conclude that more highly skilled personnel need to be deployed more rapidly during crises to prevent armed conflict, protect civilians, and enforce the law.[10] The growing recognition of need for a new UN capability has led to numerous efforts to prepare more readily available national police and military units, regional forces (e.g., NATO), voluntary forms of international collaboration (e.g., the Standby High Readiness Brigade), and *ad hoc* mechanisms (e.g., the Economic Community of West African States in Liberia and Sierra Leone). The African Union's growing interest in developing a capacity to intervene against war crimes, genocide, and crimes against humanity, and the G-8 Action Plan for Expanding Global Capacity for Peace Support Operations are also important steps.[11] Yet none of these groups will be *immediately* available. They cannot be deployed quickly because of insufficient readiness or because they require national decisions that in practice have delayed deployments. None possesses the full range and depth of competence needed. And these other forces may, in some cases, lack the legitimacy essential for eliciting financial support and enforcing measures that hold leaders accountable to international law.

In short, whether acting within or outside of the United Nations, governments have yet to develop a reliable capability for rapid action to prevent genocide, enforce peace, and transform conflicts to restore law, justice, and civil order to nations torn apart by violence. Despite widespread acknowledgment that the world needs an integrated global effort to prevent armed conflict and to protect potential victims from catastrophes, there is no agreement on what to do next. As a result, even if the international community speaks through the Security Council and agrees to act in a particular case, it still lacks the tool needed to meet the challenge. The uncertainty on how to proceed in providing a swift and effective capacity can be resolved—if enough people agree on the following proposal to create a permanent UN Emergency Peace Service.

The Proposal

Most recent humanitarian crises have demonstrated four needs: (1) to take action to prevent war and dire threats to human security and human rights; (2) to offer secure emergency services to meet critical human needs; (3) to maintain or reinstate law, order, penal, and judicial processes with high professionalism and fairness; and (4) to initiate peacebuilding processes with focused incentives to restore hope for local people that their society and economy have a future. The UN Emergency Peace Service proposed here is designed to provide a rapid response to these needs. It would possess five unique strengths:

- it would be permanent, based at UN designated sites, include mobile field headquarters, and be able to act immediately to cope with an emergency;

- it would be individually recruited from among those who volunteer from many countries so it would not suffer the delays of creating ad hoc forces or the reluctance of UN members to deploy their own national units; [12]

- its personnel would be carefully selected, expertly trained, [13] and coherently organized, so it would not fail in its mission due to a lack of skills, equipment, cohesiveness, experience in resolving conflicts, or gender, national, or religious imbalance;

- it would be a dedicated service with a wide range of professional skills within a single command structure, prepared to conduct multiple functions in diverse UN operations, enabling it to avoid divided loyalties, confusion about the chain of command, or functional fragmentation; and

- it would provide an integrated service encompassing 12,000 to 15,000 civilian, police, judicial, military, and relief professionals, enabling it to deploy all the components essential for peace and enforcement operations.

With these professional capabilities, a UN agency would, for the first time in history, offer a rapid, comprehensive, internationally legitimate response to crisis, enabling it to save hundreds of thousands of lives and billions of dollars through early and often preventive action.

Each field unit would contain sufficient strength and versatility to provide robust security as well as the necessary range of skills and services to initiate conflict transformation and the rule of law within their sphere of control while simultaneously addressing human needs. The Emergency Peace Service might deploy UN protection personnel to prevent large-scale killings, [14] a police unit to help provide safety in tense local communities and to protect those delivering humanitarian services to threatened people, and a disaster relief service. Where needed, it could also provide reliable, early, on-site fact-finding, rapid mobility for preventive action to protect civilians at risk, information-gathering for war crimes investigations, humanitarian assistance, and prompt start-up of peacebuilding operations. The UN Service would also include units to re-train and monitor local police, to conduct conflict resolution efforts, and to respond to humanitarian crises growing out of environmental or natural disasters that national governments are unable or unwilling to address.[15]

The proposed Emergency Service would be designed to complement but not to replace existing or expanded peace operations by the United Nations, regional international organizations, and national governments. Protecting people against victimization from armed conflict and gross violations of human rights may at times require more personnel than the proposed UN Emergency Peace Service could provide by itself. Moreover, because peacebuilding often requires extensive and sustained efforts, long-term success in preventing genocides and other crimes against humanity will require support from the wider UN system and complementary efforts by national and regional actors. The proposed Emergency Service might be viewed as a "first in, first out" response to a crisis, although in particular cases it might continue the deployment of some personnel, such as for training and monitoring local civilian police, after other agencies have arrived to address any needs too large and long-term for the UN Emergency Peace Service to handle by itself.

Fortunately, several recent initiatives provide the essential foundation on which to build the proposed UN Emergency Peace Service. These include the expansion of the UN Department of Peacekeeping Operations, the refinement of the UN Standby Arrangements System (UNSAS), the development of the multinational Standby High Readiness Brigade for UN peace operations (SHIRBRIG),[16] and the new strategic deployment stocks in Brindisi, Italy. For the larger tasks, further implementation of the recommendations in the Brahimi Report and regional efforts, such as those being pursued by African countries and by the European Union, are necessary. The recommendations of the High-Level Panel on Threats, Challenges, and Change and the Secretary-General's report, *In Larger Freedom: Towards Development, Security and Human Rights for All*,[17] should also be heeded. Implementation of these measures would not diminish the need for the UN Emergency Peace Service. Indeed they would enable it to function more effectively, while it, in turn, would contribute to broader goals for preventing genocide and enhancing rapid-reaction capability.

We commend the proponents of these other initiatives and offer our support for further development of these measures. Nonetheless, many officials in the United Nations and national governments recognize that some inherent limitations in these arrangements point toward the need to take further steps. Although the recent reforms enhance the UN's capacity for peacekeeping, they cannot and will not provide an assurance of rapid response to fast-breaking crises because they still depend on national deliberations, decisions, and provision of personnel. Such limitations inevitably delay response. Repeated efforts to overcome such limitations have failed, suggesting that they can be overcome only through a new institutional initiative. In short, the existing arrangements are essential and should be expanded, but they are insufficient. They will remain slower than often needed, less reliable and well-prepared than desirable, and understandably less competent than a dedicated force in carrying out delicate, specialized, multiple functions simultaneously. Indeed, the existing agencies would be able to perform their existing tasks and the measures suggested by the High-Level Panel more effectively if these tasks were carried out in tandem with the kind of professionalism proposed in a UN Emergency Peace Service. In addition, the proposed Service could help overcome existing gaps in political will and capabilities.

The Decision to Deploy

The Security Council is the first, the most legitimate, and the most likely body to authorize the UN Emergency Peace Service and to clarify the threshold criteria that would justify deploying it. But if the Security Council is unable to act because of a veto, then other forms of authorization may be desirable[18] to prevent war crimes, genocide, or crimes against humanity. The two next best alternatives to the preferred legitimacy of Security Council action are: authorization by the UN General Assembly under the Uniting for Peace Resolution,[19] or authorization by a regional international organization for intervention in one of its own member states. Even less widely viewed as legitimate, but perhaps still acceptable, would be authorization for intervention by a regional international organization in a state *not* a member of the organization, especially if the conflict affects member states, as might have happened when NATO intervened in Kosovo.[20]

The United Nations could also authorize the Secretary-General to deploy the Emergency Peace Service as a result of his or her own decision, under carefully specified conditions defined in advance by the Security Council or General Assembly. If the Secretary-General determined that those conditions were met, then he or she could immediately deploy the UN Emergency Peace Service without waiting for any other body to deliberate.[21] If such authorization did occur, the Security Council could retain its power to withdraw the Emergency Service by passing a resolution following its normal voting procedures.[22]

Regardless of the particular form of authorization, six principles, most of which have been recommended by the International Commission on Intervention and State Sovereignty, provide a useful set of standards for decision-making.[23] This framework arises from the norms contained in existing international treaties, including the UN Charter, the Genocide Convention, the Geneva Conventions, and the findings of a variety of expert commissions, as well as from traditional just war thinking. To reassure all parties who are understandably concerned about enabling *unwarranted* interventions, the following high standards should be met to justify coercive intervention: (1) a legitimate authority must authorize deployment; (2) there must be a just cause;[24] (3) intervention must be undertaken with a right intention; (4) intervention should occur only when there is an immediate and evident threat of gross violations of international humanitarian and human rights law; (5) the means employed must be proportional to and consistent with the ends sought; and (6) a reasonable prospect of success must exist.

The fourth of these guidelines reformulates the traditional standard of "last resort," which is appropriate for conventional military combat, to fit internationally authorized coercive measures of law enforcement, which reflect less a right to engage in conventional military combat than the international responsibility to protect people under severe threat. The International Commission on Intervention and State Sovereignty has noted that the requirement of last resort should not be used to delay intervention, including preventive deployments, when justified. "Last resort" needs to be understood as a restraint against *premature* use of international coercion, but "this does not necessarily mean that every . . . option must literally have been tried and failed: often there will simply not be the time for that process to work itself out."[25] When internationally authorized personnel function as much as possible in a police mode of operations to enforce international law against genocide, for example, the goal presumably would be to address the crisis at a moment *early* enough to avoid mass murder. Early deployment of law enforcers and conflict specialists to address an imminent threat of genocide not yet underway can sometimes avoid later need for more large-scale military combat. Requiring international authorization for deployment, eschewing unnecessary violence, and focusing law enforcement on *individual* rather than collective misconduct, insofar as possible, provide some reassurances against abuse of international police power.

While recognizing the wisdom and propriety of avoiding unwarranted coercive interventions, there also is a co-existing *duty* to prevent large-scale loss of life and gross violations of human rights such as genocide.[26] Because the proposed Emergency Service would, for the first time in history, enable the international community to discharge its responsibilities at the time when it can do the most good with means that exact the least moral cost—in the early stages of a crisis—it would incur fewer painful ethical dilemmas than less timely interventions which in the past have occasionally divided those emphasizing human rights from those emphasizing peace and nonviolence, thereby impeding effective restraints on the perpetrators of mass violence.

The Costs

Although the proposed UN Emergency Peace Service would entail significant financial costs, these almost certainly will be far less than the costs that will occur from conflicts allowed to fester until they spiral out of control in the absence of such a service.[27] Estimates on the cost of the UN Service vary, but start-up expenses could come to $2 billion, with an annual recurring cost of $900 million or more, depending on field operations.[28] Although this cost could be viewed initially as beyond the capacity of UN member states, such a service would reduce the number and size of other UN peace operations, help prevent armed conflicts from escalating or spreading, and reduce the high costs of prolonged operations. It is likely to be a cost-effective instrument, able to reduce the overall costs of UN peace and enforcement operations in the long run.[29] The Carnegie Commission on Preventing Deadly Conflict found that the international community "spent approximately $200 billion on conflict management in seven major interventions in the 1990s (Bosnia and Herzegovina, Somalia, Rwanda, Haiti, the Persian Gulf, Cambodia, and El Salvador)." It could have saved $130 billion of this amount "through a more effective preventive approach"[30] that a UN Emergency Peace Service would help make possible. Additional billions could have been saved by external powers that were involved directly or indirectly in the conflicts.[31] Yet if the proposed Emergency Service saved only one or two billion "conflict dollars" annually, which it almost certainly would do, it would be a cost-effective investment for saving both lives and financial resources.[32]

The Benefits

The benefits of a permanent, sophisticated UN Emergency Peace Service are clear. In past crises, the UN has often been unable to assemble personnel and provide assistance in less than three to six months. Even then these *ad hoc* forces were not always well prepared for their demanding tasks. The proposed UN Service would directly surmount these difficulties and also lift the burden that now makes governments reluctant to deploy their own national citizens in conflicts with high risk and low national interest. As a dedicated UN Service with personnel recruited from among carefully selected volunteers, it would no longer need to acquire the last-minute approval of or meet the conditions imposed by each member state that participates in a conventional peacekeeping operation. Life-saving decisions for international help would be easier for the Security Council to make. The UN Service could also play a constructive preventive role during crises when mass violence might otherwise appear tempting to some. If cynical political leaders in strife-ridden societies knew that a rapid reaction UN Service could be deployed quickly to enforce international law, some of those political leaders who otherwise might be tempted to commit misdeeds would be more likely to be deterred. As Secretary-General Annan put it, "If states bent on criminal behavior know that frontiers are not the absolute defence; if they know that the Security Council will take action to halt crimes against humanity, then they will not embark on such a course of action in expectation of sovereignty impunity."[33]

The UN Emergency Peace Service could also help where a government would *consent* to the deployment of UN personnel, rather than be forced to accept them, either as a result of pressure from the Security Council or because a government wanted UN help to prevent its society from sliding into chaos and genocide. The Indonesian government, for example, eventually accepted a multinational force to keep peace in East Timor for two reasons. First, the Security Council pressed for acceptance and the office of the Secretary-General let members of the government know that they might face criminal responsibility for their inability to stop violence if it was also accompanied by their continued refusal to accept proffered UN help. Second, an *ad hoc* UN interventionary force, with Australian help, actually existed and stood at the ready. A permanent UN Emergency Peace Service could play a similar deterring role even earlier and more effectively,[34] thereby helping to elicit consent for a UN deployment. Such a Service would increase the willingness of both the Security Council to deploy and a state to give consent to a UN presence, thereby doubly facilitating UN prevention of mass murder and possibly war.

Of course a UN Emergency Peace Service would be no panacea; it would not have worked well in every one of the conflicts since the end of the Cold War. Yet even in crises that might turn out to be too large for the proposed Service to manage, it could play a vital role in enhancing the effectiveness of other UN and regional capabilities, serving first as a rapid-reaction team to avert a spiral toward social break-down and subsequently as an advance party preparing the way for later deployment of other capabilities.

Moreover, a conflict that in retrospect might appear to have been beyond the capacity of a small emergency service might have been amenable to successful intervention if it had occurred in an early preventive phase of a conflict's life cycle. Increasingly, governments understand that early preventive action is more effective and less costly than later, larger efforts after a conflict has escalated and spread. The capacity to respond rapidly is often crucial for preventing bloodshed that, once begun, may tear the social fabric forever beyond repair.

If it had existed in the 1990s, such a capacity could have prevented untold destruction and suffering while reducing or eliminating the high costs of post-conflict reconstruction after a society and its supportive infrastructure have been devastated by violent conflict. Instead of waiting for weeks or even months for national assistance to respond to a UN call, the UN would have the option to deploy its own discrete Service immediately, with highly trained personnel, operating with a clear chain of command responsibility, using the best equipment available, and possessing the highest overall competence and legitimacy to prevent atrocities.

The Call to Action

Many leaders from scores of national governments, the United Nations, regional organizations, human rights organizations, religious groups, and surviving members of victimized families around the world are calling for a rapid deployment capability to protect the innocent from further atrocities.[35] There are encouraging signs of support for developing such a capacity in the African Union, in the European Union, among progressive governments elsewhere, and in public opinion from every corner of the world.[36] But because governments have not answered this call, responsibility for breathing life into a United Nations Emergency Peace Service now lies with members of civil society, in cooperation with the United Nations, regional organizations, and governments wherever possible. With support from those convinced of the need to end genocide and other crimes, an Emergency Service *can* be created, and sooner rather than later.

The next step in establishing a UN Emergency Peace Service is to build widespread, well-informed political influence by expanding the network of supportive parties. Help will be needed from diverse sectors of civil society, particularly NGOs, foundations, and academe. Determined efforts by a global constituency are required. Fortunately, such a constituency already has leaders who are experienced in transnational politics, because this proposal builds upon and links the previous work of many people, including efforts such as the Panel on UN Peace Operations (Brahimi Report),[37] the report of the International Commission on Intervention and State Sovereignty, the High-Level Panel on Threats, Challenges, and Change, and the other path-breaking initiatives to enhance UN rapid deployment, to emphasize preventive measures, to de-legitimize and remove anti-personnel land mines, and to establish the permanent International Criminal Court.

To succeed in creating this life-sustaining UN Emergency Peace Service, a growing number of citizens' organizations and leaders of civil society are determined to implement these essential steps:

(1) identify interested parties throughout the world to establish a large, diverse, well-organized network of support;

(2) draw on expert knowledge to ensure that the growing constituency is well informed and to provide a more detailed vision of how to establish an effective Emergency Peace Service;

(3) secure agreement, after full consultation, on the principles, composition, and financing of a preferred model for the UN

Emergency Peace Service;

(4) develop a compelling website, well-researched studies on all major issues, solid promotional materials showing the costs and benefits of the proposal, an expanding list of endorsements, and an expert speakers' bureau, coordinated from agreed institutional homes; and

(5) encourage wide consultative and networking processes among non-governmental organizations, the UN system, and national governments to shape and implement a successful strategy.[38]

The creation of a United Nations Emergency Peace Service will produce enough true benefits for all countries to demonstrate that, when it comes to stopping genocide and crimes against humanity, "the collective interest *is* the national interest." [39] The proposed UN Service could curtail violence in divided societies, deflect venomous attacks between those of different identities and religious traditions, end a culture of impunity, encourage the concentration of scarce resources on meeting human needs rather than on harming one's neighbors, and bring an energizing focus to the meaning of common, human security. It could produce monumental benefits in lives saved, mothers and daughters protected against grievous violations, families still able to live at home, time and money never spent to kill and destroy, tolerance maintained, laws upheld, and communities at peace. By acting together we can enliven that spark of human solidarity that lives, too often hidden, within people everywhere on earth. *Finally*, we can give genuine meaning to "Never again."

Endnotes

[1]This essay was written by Robert C. Johansen on behalf of the Working Group for a United Nations Emergency Peace Service. It is based in part on an early draft by H. Peter Langille and on comments from members of the Working Group. This proposal grew out of a symposium on "Genocide and Crimes Against Humanity: The Challenge of Prevention and Enforcement," co-sponsored by the Nuclear Age Peace Foundation; the Simons Centre for Peace and Disarmament Studies, Liu Institute for Global Issues, University of British Columbia; Global Action to Prevent War; and the Law and Society Program, University of California, Santa Barbara, December 5-6, 2003. Parts of this essay draw on the initial concept, case, model, and plans for a United Nations Emergency Service developed by H. Peter Langille, and discussed in his *Bridging the Commitment-Capacity Gap: A Review of Existing Arrangements and Options for Enhancing UN Rapid Deployment* (Wayne, NJ: Center for UN Reform Education, 2002). This essay also builds on earlier work to develop UN rapid deployment capabilities for preventing armed conflict and protecting civilians in emergencies, including William R. Frye, *A United Nations Peace Force* (New York: Oceana Publications, 1957); Robert C. Johansen and Saul H. Mendlovitz, "The Role of Enforcement of Law in the Establishment of a New International Order: A Proposal for a Transnational Police Force," *Alternatives: A Journal of World Policy* 6 (1980): 307-338; Robert C. Johansen, "UN Peacekeeping and the Changing Utility of Military Force," *Third World Quarterly* 12 (1990): 53-70; Brian Urquhart, "For a UN Volunteer Military Force," *New York Review of Books* 40 (10 June 1993): 3-4; Howard Peter Langille, James Hammond, and Carleton Hughes, "A Preliminary Blueprint of Long-Term Options for Enhancing a United Nations Rapid Reaction Capability" in David Cox and Albert Legault (eds.), *UN Rapid Reaction Capabilities: Requirements and Prospects* (Cornwallis: The Pearson Peacekeeping Press, 1995); Robert C. Johansen, "Enhancing United Nations Peacekeeping" in Chadwick F. Alger (ed.), *The Future of the United Nations System: Potential for the Twenty-first Century* (Tokyo: The United Nations University Press, 1998), 89-126; Howard Peter Langille, "Conflict Prevention: Options for Rapid Deployment and UN Standing Forces," Special Issue of *International Peacekeeping*, Tom Woodhouse and Oliver Ramsbotham (eds.) 7 (2000): 219-253 [reprinted in Oliver Ramsbotham and Tom Woodhouse (eds.), *Peacekeeping As Conflict Resolution* (London: Frank Cass Publishers, 2000)]; and Saul Mendlovitz and John Fousek, "A UN Constabulary to Enforce the Law on Genocide and Crimes Against Humanity," in Neil Reimer (ed.), *Protection Against Genocide: Mission Impossible?* (London: Praeger, 2000), 105-122.

[2]Kofi Annan said: "We are living through a crisis of the international system" calling into question "whether the institutions and methods we are accustomed to are really adequate. . . ." Quoted in Felicity Barringer, "Annan Warns of World 'Crisis,'" *New York Times*, 31 July 2003, A 16.

[3]With the UN report on Srebrenica and the Independent Inquiry on Rwanda, Kofi Annan acknowledged UN failures, expressed his own deep remorse, and said, "Of all my aims as Secretary-General, there is none to which I feel more deeply committed than that of enabling the United Nations never again to fail in protecting a civilian population from genocide or mass slaughter." *Report of the Independent Inquiry into the Actions of the United Nations* and *Srebrenica: Report of the Fall of Srebrenica*, UN Document A54/549, 15 November, 1999.

[4]See H. Peter Langille, *Bridging the Commitment-Capacity Gap. . .* ; Saul Mendlovitz and John Fousek, "A UN Constabulary to Enforce the Law. . . ."

[5]Because the UN emergency service is focused on averting widespread loss of life, if deployment were to occur in connection with an environmental disaster, it would occur only after recognition by the appropriate authorizing body that the disaster was so severe as to extend beyond the capacity of a state and other relevant international organizations to address it and likely to result in a state's fundamental failure to protect many of its own people, either because it was unable or unwilling to do so.

[6]Francis M. Deng, the Representative of the Secretary-General on Internally Displaced Persons and a former Sudanese diplomat, has articulated this concept in reconciling sovereign immunity from external intervention with international responsibility to intervene, by adding to the three traditional attributes of sovereignty (territory, a people, and governmental authority), a fourth characteristic: respect for a minimal standard of human rights. Francis M. Deng, *Protecting the Dispossessed: A Challenge for the International Community* (Washington, D.C.: Brookings Institution, 1993); Francis M. Deng et al., *Sovereignty as Responsibility* (Washington, D.C.: Brookings Institution, 1995); and Francis M. Deng, "Frontiers of Sovereignty," *Leiden Journal of International Law* 8 (1995): 249-286; Roberta Cohen and Francis M. Deng, *Masses in Flight: The Global Crisis in Displacement* (Washington, D.C.: Brookings Institution, 1998).

Former Secretary-General Boutros Boutros-Ghali earlier recognized the changing boundaries of sovereignty when he wrote "The centuries-old doctrine of absolute and exclusive sovereignty no longer stands. . . . A major intellectual requirement of our time is to rethink the question of sovereignty." Boutros Boutros-Ghali, "Empowering the United Nations," *Foreign Affairs* 72 (Winter 1992-1993): 98-99.

Secretary-General Kofi Annan observed that "state sovereignty, in its most basic sense, is being redefined. . . . States are now widely understood to be instruments at the service of their peoples, and not vice versa. At the same time, individual sovereignty—by which I mean the fundamental freedom of each individual, enshrined in the charter of the UN and subsequent international treaties—has been enhanced by a renewed and spreading consciousness of individual rights. . . ." He said "we should welcome" the "developing international norm in favour of intervention to protect civilians from wholesale slaughter. . . ." Kofi Annan, "Two Concepts of Sovereignty," *The Economist* 352 (18 September 1999): 49-50. Annan earlier said "The Charter protects the sovereignty of peoples. It was never meant as a license for governments to trample on human rights and human dignity. Sovereignty implies responsibility, not just power." See "Reflections on Intervention," Ditchley Foundation Lecture 26 June, 1998, reprinted in *The Question of Intervention: Statements by the Secretary-General* (New York: United Nations, 1999), 6. See also Kofi Annan, "Secretary-General's Speech to the 54th Session of the General Assembly," September 20, 1999; and *Report of the Secretary-General on the Work of the Organization*, Document A/54/1.

[7]Kofi Annan, "Two Concepts of Sovereignty," 49-50.

[8]Kofi Annan, "Secretary-General's Annual Report to the General Assembly," *UN Press Release,* 20 September 1999: 2.

[9]The International Commission on Intervention and State Sovereignty observed that "If by its actions and, indeed, crimes, a state destroys the lives and rights of its citizens, it forfeits temporarily its moral claim to be treated as legitimate. Its sovereignty, as well as its right to nonintervention is suspended." International Commission on Intervention and State Sovereignty, *The Responsibility to Protect* (Ottawa, Canada: International Development Research Centre, 2001), 136; 5-13. See also Ramesh Thakur, "Global Norms and International Humanitarian Law: An Asian Perspective," *International Review of the Red Cross,* 83, no. 841 (March 2001): 35.

[10]See, for example, Government of Canada, *Towards A Rapid Deployment Capability for the United Nations, Report by the Government of Canada* (1995); Robert C. Johansen, "The Future of United Nations Peacekeeping and Enforcement: A Framework for Policymaking," *Global Governance* 2, no. 3 (September-December 1996): 299-333; Stephen P. Kinloch, "Utopian or Pragmatic? A UN Permanent Military Volunteer Force," *International Peacekeeping* 3 (Winter 1996); Brian Urquhart and Francois Heisbourg, "Prospects for a Rapid Response Capability: A Dialogue," in *Peacemaking and Peacekeeping for the New Century*, ed. Olara Otunnu and Michael W. Doyle (Lanham, MD: Rowman & Littlefield Publishers, 1998), 189-99; William J. Durch, *Discussion of the Report of the Panel On UN Peace Operations: The Brahimi Report* (The Stimson Center, 2000); Howard Peter Langille, "Renewing Partnerships for the Prevention of Armed Conflict: Options to Enhance Rapid Deployment and Initiate A UN Standing Emergency Capability," Canadian Centre for Foreign Policy Development and the DFAIT (June 2000), http://www.worldfederalistscanada.org/langille1.pdf; United Nations, "Report of the Panel on United Nations Peace Operations," http://www.un.org/peace/reports/peaceoperations/docs/a55305.pdf, A/55/305-S/2000/809; John G. Heidenrich, *How to Prevent Genocide: A Guide for Policymakers, Scholars and the Concerned Citizen* (Westport: Praeger, 2001); Challenges Project, *Challenges of Peace Operations: Into the 21st Century, Concluding Report* (Stockholm: Elanders Gotab, 2002); William

J. Durch, Victoria K. Holt, Caroline R. Earle, Moira K. Shanahan, *The Brahimi Report and the Future of UN Peace Operations* (Washington, D.C.: Henry L. Stimson Center Report, 2003), http://www.stimson.org/pubs.cfm?ID=90.

[11]See African Union Constitutive Act, Art. 4(h); and *G8 Action Plan for Expanding Global Capacity for Peace Support Operations*, http://www.g8usa.gov/pdfs/0610ActionPlan PeaceOperations.pdf.

[12]More than a sufficient number of dedicated, skilled individuals are to likely volunteer for this professional service [See the Commission on Global Governance, *Our Global Neighborhood* (New York: Oxford University Press, 1995), 112]. They would be paid on a full-time basis as are other UN civil servants. Applicants would be encouraged from all member states to encourage universal representation.

[13]Training would focus not only on expertise within a person's primary functional area of responsibility, but also on international human rights law and the laws of war.

[14]Although the proposed UN service would not be a large force designed to conduct major military combat, it must have a sufficient enforcement capability to maintain security and safety for the people within its area of operations. If armed personnel are deployed in sufficient numbers, they often are able to operate more in a police mode than in a combat role even if they are military personnel. In most of the tense incidents in Kosovo following the cease-fire agreement, for example, this was true of the NATO role, where 40,000 soldiers were deployed.

[15]On the unrealized potential of UN civilian police, see Robert C. Johansen, "Enforcing Norms and Normalizing Enforcement for Humane Governance," in *Principled World Politics: The Challenge of Normative International Relations*, edited by Paul Wapner and Lester Edwin J. Ruiz (New York: Rowman & Littlefield, 2000), 218-227. For a detailed list of required units, see H.P. Langille, *Bridging the Commitment-Capacity Gap . . .* , 128.

[16]For analysis of the SHIRBRIG, see H.P. Langille, "La Brigade multinationale d'intervention rapide des forces en attente des Nations Unies (BIRFA): est-elle perfectible?" in Jocelyn Coulon (ed.), *Guide du maintien de la pais* (Outrement: Athena Publications, 2004), 111-126.

[17]The panel said the Security Council needs "to be prepared to be more proactive in the future, taking decisive action earlier." If a state fails in its "responsibility to protect its civilians from large-scale violence," then "the international community . . . has a further responsibility to act. . . ." See "A More Secure World: Our Shared Responsibility," *Report of the Secretary-General's High-level Panel on Threats, Challenges and Change* (New York: United Nations, 2004), 4; A/59/565, 2 December 2004; available at http://www.un.org/secureworld/report.pdf, accessed December 13, 2004. See also

UN Secretary-General, Report to the General Assembly, March 21, 2005, available at http://www.un.org/largerfreedom/.

[18]The Working Group for a UN Emergency Peace Service agrees with the International Commission on Intervention and State Sovereignty that a higher emphasis should be placed on making the Security Council work better than on developing alternatives to the Security Council as a source of authority, although the latter may be needed if the Council is paralyzed by a veto. See International Commission on Intervention and State Sovereignty, *The Responsibility to Protect*, 49.

[19]United Nations General Assembly, "General Assembly Resolution 377A, November 3, 1950 (V)," in *Charter Review Documents*, 557-61.

[20]For discussion of these issues, see International Commission on Intervention and State Sovereignty, *The Responsibility to Protect*, 53-55.

[21]For comment on this approach, see Saul Mendlovitz and John Fousek, "Enforcing the Law on Genocide," *Alternatives* 21(1996): 253.

[22]A veto could prevent passage of a withdrawal resolution, thereby leaving the Secretary-General with the right to keep the emergency service in place if he or she chose to do so.

[23]International Commission on Intervention and State Sovereignty, *The Responsibility to Protect*, 31-37.

[24]"Just cause" is associated with coercive responses to prevent crimes against humanity, genocide, war crimes specified in the Geneva conventions and protocols; suffering caused by state collapse and resultant starvation, civil war, and gross violations of human rights; and overwhelming natural or environmental catastrophes where the state is unable or unwilling to prevent severe humanitarian crisis. See *The Responsibility to Protect*, 32.

[25]See International Commission on Intervention and State Sovereignty, *The Responsibility to Protect*, 36.

[26]The duty to prevent is clearly stated in the Genocide Convention, Article 1. See also *The Responsibility to Protect*, xi-xiii.

[27]In the "Secretary-General's Annual Report to the General Assembly," Kofi Annan said, "Even the costliest policy of prevention is far cheaper, in lives and in resources, than the least expensive use of armed force." "UN Press Release," September 20, 1999, www.globalpolicy.org/secgen/sg-ga.htm, accessed July 29, 2004.

[28]Even if annual expenditures amounted to $3 billion, for the United States to pay

25 percent of the costs would amount to only about $2 for each U.S. citizen. Other industrialized countries would pay $1 to $2 per capita. The per capita cost for poor countries would be less than 10 cents. These amounts could be placed in the regular UN budget assessments. Alternatively, the emergency force could be funded from small levies on the weapons trade, military budgets, or international currency exchanges if the international community should decide to do so.

[29]For further cost-benefit analysis of a UN emergency service, see Langille, *Bridging the Commitment–Capacity Gap . . .* , 75-114.

[30]International Commission on Intervention and State Sovereignty, *The Responsibility to Protect,* 20. See also Carnegie Commission on Preventing Deadly Conflict, *The Costs of Conflict: Prevention and Cure in the Global Arena,* eds. Michael E. Brown and Richard N. Rosecrane (Lanham, Md: Rowman & Littlefield, 1999).

[31]Secretary-General Annan emphasized the economy of prevention when he noted that the premature withdrawal of UN peacekeepers by the international community, no less than when it unreasonably delays a deployment, "can be costly in both financial and human terms," because dealing with the aftermath of genocide costs much more than preventing it. The cost of reinforcing UNAMIR in Rwanda, for example, with the 5,000 soldiers that UN commander General Romeo Dallaire "thought were needed to prevent or stop the genocide has been estimated at $500 million; the cost of humanitarian assistance to Rwanda and the region consequent on the genocide was in excess of $4.5 billion." See United Nations Security Council, Report of the Secretary-General, "No Exit Without Strategy: Security Council Decision-making and the Closure or Transition of United Nations Peacekeeping Operations," S/2001/394 (April 20, 2001): 5-6. http://www.globalpolicy.org/security/peacekpg/reform/2001/0420sgreport.pdf, accessed 13 January 2005.

[32]Irwin Cotler reported to the Stockholm International Forum on Preventing Genocide that "trite as it is profound," the "best protection against mass atrocity is the prevention of the 'killing fields' to begin with." The international community "spent eight times more dealing with the aftermath of conflict and genocide than it invested in the prevention of it." The full cost of genocide "is incalculable." See "Address by the Honourable Irwin Cotler, Minister of Justice and Attorney General of Canada for the Stockholm International Forum," Stockholm International Forum on Preventing Genocide: Threats and Responsibilities, Sweden, January 26, 2004, http://www.preventinggenocide.com/files/Canada_eng.pdf, accessed July 27, 2004.

[33]Kofi Annan, "Secretary-General's Annual Report to the General Assembly," *UN Press Release*, 20 September 1999: 5.

[34]The Commission on Global Governance concluded that "the very existence of an

immediately available and effective UN Volunteer Force could be a deterrent in itself. ... As its skill, experience, and reputation grew, its need to use force would probably decrease. .... It is high time that this idea—A United Nations Volunteer Force—was made a reality." The Commission on Global Governance, *Our Global Neighborhood*, 112.

[35]See, for example, Erskine Childers and Brian Urquhart, *Towards a More Effective United Nations* (Uppsala: Dag Hammarskjold Foundation, 1992); Commission on Global Governance, *Our Global Neighborhood*; Carnegie Commission on Preventing Deadly Conflict, *Preventing Deadly Conflict* (Washington, D.C.: Carnegie Commission on Preventing Deadly Conflict, 1997); Neal Riemer, *Protection Against Genocide* (Westport, CN: Praeger, 2000); John Heidenrich, *How to Prevent Genocide: A Guide for Policymakers, Scholars and the Concerned Citizen* (Westport: Praeger, 2001).

[36]See, for example, the opinion polling done by the Program on International Policy Attitudes at the Center for the Study of Policy Attitudes and the Center for International and Security Studies at the School of Public Affairs, University of Maryland. Data as early as the 1990s showed 79 percent of the U.S. public favored improving UN rapid deployment capabilities. Summary data is reported at the Council for a Livable World Education Fund, http://www.clw.org/un/unpol96.html, accessed August 10, 2004.

[37]Scholars at the Stimson Center are following these and related reforms. See www.stimson.org/fopo.

[38]H. P. Langille, "Overview of Current UN Efforts: Enforcement, Rapid Deployment, Protection of Civilians and the Prevention of Armed Conflict," paper presented at the symposium, "Genocide and Crimes Against Humanity: The Challenge of Prevention and Enforcement," University of California, Santa Barbara (December 5, 2003), 19.

[39]Kofi Annan, "Two Concepts of Sovereignty," 49. Emphasis added.

3

EXPERT DISCUSSION OF THE UNITED NATIONS EMERGENCY PEACE SERVICE: THE CUENCA REPORT

Robert C. Johansen, Rapporteur

Introduction

Thirty-five experts drawn from all major cultural regions of the world met at the University of Castilla–La Mancha in Cuenca, Spain, February 5-6, 2005, for the purpose of discussing two main questions: (1) What are the merits of establishing a permanent United Nations emergency capability to protect people from genocide, war crimes, and crimes against humanity? (2) What are the possibilities for building sufficient worldwide political support to establish such a service?[1]

The participants examined the proposal for a United Nations Emergency Peace Service (UNEPS), which is detailed in the previous chapter, by bringing diverse national, cultural, scholarly, and ideological vantage points to the analysis. Formal discussions and informal conversations clarified points of agreement and disagreement on key substantive issues and laid a preliminary foundation for establishing future political cooperation that could provide the leaven in an expanding political project dedicated to building a new international institution to protect innocent people from heinous crimes.

All participants, without exception, agreed that the international community urgently needs an effective United Nations rapid reaction capability if it is to honor its responsibility to protect innocent people from genocide, war crimes, and crimes against humanity. Participants also agreed that the

UNEPS proposal for a permanent, individually-recruited group of highly trained professionals should be the focus of future efforts.

What follows is a summary of the substantive discussions of experts in the Cuenca meetings, supplemented by subsequent conversations with additional experts, organized around major subjects of debate to facilitate the further development of the UNEPS proposal. Points of agreement or disagreement are highlighted in preparation for refinements that will be incorporated into the proposal after further discussion. Following the present introduction, this report briefly explains the goals for the Cuenca discussions and provides an overview of the proposal for a United Nations Emergency Peace Service. Next the report explores fundamental questions, followed by more specific or technical issues. The report then describes the principles on which participants come to agreement, followed by a list of topics where further analysis and discussion are needed. The report concludes with factors that should shape the future strategy for establishing the UN Emergency Peace Service and a call for organizational endorsements.

Goals of the Cuenca Discussions

The three main goals for the meetings were: (1) to develop an effective and politically feasible proposal for a UN rapid response capability; (2) to ensure worldwide participation in formulating the proposal; and (3) to build consensus for advancing a common proposal. To widen participation while simultaneously pushing for deeper consensus is always a challenge, but in this case the opportunity to hear one another's views face-to-face enabled progress on both. In a few areas where disagreement persisted, all of the participants genuinely respected each others' views. The diverse participation and substantive agreement nurtured at Cuenca reflect significant progress toward opening the door to enforcement by legitimate global authority of international laws prohibiting genocide, war crimes, and crimes against humanity. UNEPS can institutionalize change that will help to deter these crimes, to stop them when they occur, and also to discourage war. We now have the basis for advancing a proposal that reflects broadly compatible perspectives and the design for a UN Emergency Peace Service that, we believe, is politically feasible as well as morally necessary. We have consensus on the basic principles for a UN Emergency Peace Service.

Overview of a United Nations Emergency Peace Service

The meeting opened with a discussion of the rationale for a United Nations Emergency Peace Service and the areas of possible agreement and disagreement.

The Need

Despite the need, the United Nations has no reliable capability to deploy a security operation promptly, even if halting a catastrophe might save hundreds of thousands of lives. Massive killings of innocent people have illustrated this incapacity in Rwanda, Cambodia, the former Yugoslavia, East Timor, Sierra Leone, the Democratic Republic of the Congo, Liberia, Sudan, and elsewhere.

Rather than allow such killings to happen, by creating a permanent UN Emergency Peace Service we can ensure that the next preventable humanitarian disaster will not occur. If such a service had been established earlier, it could have prevented many of the atrocities that have killed and wounded millions of civilians, forced tens of millions from their homes, destroyed entire economies, and wasted hundreds of billions of dollars. Of course such a service would not be a panacea for security problems in general; indeed it would be designed to complement—not replace—other essential national, regional, and United Nations efforts. Yet a UN Emergency Service could provide immediate, full protection in some crises and serve as an advance group that would prepare the way for subsequent additional help, if needed, in larger conflicts. This would fulfill a vital function that is not provided by any other existing or anticipated agency. Such a service could also help address extreme environmental and natural disasters in cases where other remedies are inadequate for averting major threats to human life.

The Proposal

1.   The UN Emergency Peace Service should be **permanent** and based at UN designated sites.

2.   It should be capable of **immediate response** so it could quell an emergency within 24 to 48 hours after United Nations authorization.

3.   It should be **individually recruited** from among volunteers drawn from many countries.

4.   The 12,000 to 15,000 personnel recruited should be **carefully selected** and **expertly trained**, with sensitivity to implementing UN Resolution 1325 regarding women's human rights.

5.   The proposed Service should be **coherently organized** and under a **unified UN command**.

6.   It should provide **diverse services** within an integrated force structure, encompassing civilians skilled in conflict resolution, humanitarian assistance, human rights, police enforcement, judicial processes, and military personnel.

Each field unit would contain sufficient strength and versatility to provide robust security as well as the necessary range of skills and services to initiate conflict transformation and the rule of law within their sphere of control while simultaneously addressing emergency human needs.

The growing recognition of need for a new UN capability has led to numerous efforts to prepare more readily available national police and military units, regional forces (e.g., NATO, European Union (EU) battle groups, African Union peacekeeping forces), voluntary forms of international collaboration (e.g., the UN Standby High Readiness Brigade), and *ad hoc* mechanisms (e.g., the Economic Community of West African States in Liberia and Sierra Leone). The African Union's growing interest in developing a capacity to intervene against war crimes, genocide, and crimes against humanity, and the G-8 Action Plan for Expanding Global Capacity for Peace Support Operations are also important steps. Yet none of these groups will be *immediately* available and in most cases they do not possess the full range and depth of competence needed.

The Decision to Deploy

The Working Group considered five different modes of authorization for deploying the Service, presented in the order that the Rapporteur assumed would be decreasing levels of certainty about their desirability.

1.   First, Security Council authorization would be the most legitimate justification for sending the Emergency Peace Service into action. The Security Council should clarify the threshold criteria that would generally justify deploying it.

2.   However, if the Security Council is unable to act because of a veto, then other forms of authorization may be desirable. The second line of authorization should be the UN General Assembly acting through the Uniting for Peace Resolution or possibly a General Assembly Peace Committee.

3.   Third, the Secretary-General could be authorized in advance to deploy the Emergency Peace Service as a result of his or her own decision, if carefully specified conditions defined in advance by the Security Council or General Assembly had been met. If the Secretary-General determined that those conditions existed, as presumably they would have in Rwanda in 1994, then the Secretary-General could immediately have deployed the UN Emergency Peace Service without waiting for any other body to deliberate. If such authorization did occur, the Security Council would retain its power to withdraw the Emergency Service, if it chose do so, by passing a resolution following its normal voting procedures.

4.   Fourth, a regional international organization could authorize the UN Emergency Peace Service to intervene in one of the member States of the regional organization.

5.   Fifth, a regional international organization could authorize deployment in a state *not* a member of the organization, especially if the conflict affects member states, as might have happened when NATO intervened in Kosovo.

Regardless of the particular mode of authorization, there are six principles that should be met before deployment:

1.   A legitimate authority must authorize deployment;

2.   There must be a just cause for intervention;

3.   Intervention must be undertaken with a right intention;

4.   Intervention may occur only when there is an evident threat of gross violations of international humanitarian and human rights law;

5.   The means employed must be proportional to and consistent with the ends sought; and

6.   A reasonable prospect of success must exist.

The fourth of these guidelines reformulates the traditional just war standard of "last resort,"[2] which is an appropriate standard for initiating conventional military combat. But in conducting coercive law enforcement on behalf of the international community, the last-resort standard takes on a different meaning. It should be understood as a restraint against premature use of international coercion. When internationally authorized personnel are functioning as much as possible in a police mode of operations for the purpose of enforcing international law against genocide, for example, no military action against UN forces could legitimately occur. The international community's goal presumably should be to address the crisis at a moment *early* enough to avoid mass murder. For this purpose early deployment might be better than late. There are three reassurances against abuse of coercive international police power that does not wait for literal "last resort": international authorization is required for deployment (a single government could not authorize coercive deployment); the UN personnel would be required to avoid unnecessary violence and their goal would be protecting victims in accord with well-recognized international law; and the law enforcement would emphasize *individual responsibility* more than collective guilt for misconduct.

The Costs

Although the proposed UN Emergency Peace Service would entail significant financial costs, these almost certainly will be far less than the costs that will occur from conflicts allowed to fester until they spiral out of control in the absence of such a service. Estimates on the cost of the proposed UN Service vary, but start-up expenses could come to $2 billion, with an annual recurring cost of $900 million or more, depending on field operations. Although this cost could be viewed initially as beyond the capacity of UN member states, such a service would reduce the number and size of other UN peace operations and humanitarian assistance programs, help prevent armed conflicts from spreading, and reduce the high costs of prolonged operations. The Carnegie Commission on Preventing Deadly Conflict found that the international community "spent approximately $200 billion on conflict management in seven major interventions in the 1990s (Bosnia and Herzegovina, Somalia, Rwanda, Haiti, the Persian Gulf, Cambodia, and El Salvador)." It could have saved $130 billion of this amount "through a more effective preventive approach"[3] that a UN Emergency Peace Service would help make possible.

The Benefits

The proposed UN Emergency Peace Service is designed to surmount past problems of UN peace operations, such as delayed deployments, inadequate training, and diffuse command structure, while also reducing the reluctance of governments to deploy their own national citizens in conflicts with high risk and low national interest. A dedicated UN Service with personnel recruited from among carefully selected volunteers would no longer need to acquire the approval of individual contributing countries to deploy; nor would it need to meet the operational conditions sometimes imposed by member states that contribute national contingents.

Because UNEPS would have all the life-protecting skills needed in one immediately deployable package, its availability could play a constructive preventive role during crises when mass violence threatens. If people contemplating criminal behavior "know that the Security Council will take action to halt crimes against humanity, then they will not embark on such a course of action in expectation of sovereignty impunity."[4]

The UN Emergency Peace Service could also be helpful in encouraging a government to *consent* to the deployment of UN personnel in some cases, rather than be *forced* to accept them under Chapter VII procedures, either as a result of pressure from the Security Council or because a government wanted UN help to prevent its society from sliding into chaos. A permanent, reputable Service would increase the willingness of both the Security Council to deploy and a state to give consent to a UN presence, thereby doubly facilitating UN prevention of mass murder and possibly war.

Once deployed, UNEPS could also provide on-site fact-finding, rapid mobility for preventive action to protect civilians at risk, data-gathering for war crimes investigations, humanitarian aid, and initial peacebuilding operations, including units to re-train and monitor local police, as well as to conduct conflict resolution.

The creation of a United Nations Emergency Peace Service will produce enough benefits for all countries to demonstrate that, when it comes to stopping genocide and crimes against humanity, "the collective interest *is* the national interest."[5] The proposed UN Service could curtail violence in divided societies, end a culture of impunity, encourage the concentration of scarce resources on meeting human needs rather than on harming one's neighbors, and bring an energizing focus to the meaning of common, human security. It could produce monumental benefits in lives saved, mothers and daughters protected against grievous violations, families still able to live at home, time and money never spent to kill and destroy, tolerance maintained, laws upheld, and communities at peace. By acting together, UNEPS supporters around the world can enliven that spark of human solidarity that lives, too often hidden, within many people everywhere on earth. Concerned citizens everywhere can give life-saving meaning to "Never again."

Fundamental Questions

Is the Proposal for UNEPS Politically Feasible?

The single biggest impediment to establishing a more effective UN rapid-reaction capability, participants at Cuenca agreed, is lack of political support for doing so, despite widespread recognition of the need for enhanced UN capability. Political opposition arises from the most powerful states because, much of the time at least, they do not want the United Nations itself to be strengthened. Several members of the High-level Panel on Threats, Challenges and Change, for example, reportedly favored a standing force, but when one member from a powerful country said the idea was "simply not realistic," that ended further discussion of it. Some countries in the Global South, on the other hand, fear that UNEPS could become an instrument by which the great powers would leverage their interests against weaker countries. The widespread belief that a standing or permanent force is not feasible becomes a negative self-fulfilling prophecy.

Proponents of a UN Emergency Peace Service need to tailor the proposal to address any legitimate concerns of both North and South, while watching for political opportunities to implement it. The optimal moment is likely to be one in which the great powers would, because of immediate needs, find a UNEPS helpful for protecting peace, human rights, and humanitarian assistance, while the Global South would find the structure, purpose, administration, and resources of UNEPS in harmony with their legitimate interests. Such situations do arise, as illustrated by East Timor in 1999 and Darfur in 2004-06.

Both North and South will also need to be convinced that scarce resources can be saved by making international law enforcement less of an *ad hoc* matter and by institutionalizing positive precedents for protecting innocent people against victimization. To increase the political feasibility of UNEPS it will also be necessary to mobilize citizens' organizations, especially those protecting human rights and promoting humanitarian assistance, by showing how they would benefit from the presence of UNEPS.

These considerations should be kept in mind to enhance the feasibility of the proposal:

- For some countries, it is necessary to address concerns about neo-imperialist influence or negative forces of globalization lurking behind a global enforcement capability. More could be said in the proposal to address this apprehension about the principles that should guide deployment of UNEPS in a state not consenting to its deployment.

- States in which UNEPS might intervene need reassurances regarding the conditions for withdrawal.

- For the underrepresented countries of the world, support for UNEPS would grow if they anticipated fairer forms of representation in the Security Council, since it would have the authority to use UNEPS.

- For some countries, support for UNEPS would be more likely if they were assured that the only party allowed to authorize coercive intervention would be the United Nations. Some states, for example, would like reassurances that NATO would not too readily justify its own use of force for interventionary goals, especially outside its own membership. They would not want NATO or other regional organizations to be able to authorize or direct UNEPS.

- Cooperation among countries like India, South Africa, and Brazil could be enormously important in strengthening international capability for a UN Emergency Peace Service. Such countries can connect debates that need to be brought together on poverty, health, UN reform, threats to security, and protection of people likely to be victimized by predatory forces. Such countries can play an enormously important role in their three respective continents as well as in a broader cooperative effort to advance an agenda of global reform.

How Can UNEPS Help Fulfill the Responsibility to Protect?

The credibility of efforts to create UNEPS, and its own reputation after it is established, will be influenced by the extent to which those supporting UNEPS focus on strengthening the rule of law in international relations. If in its infancy UNEPS would engage in political adventurism or fail to be impartial in enforcement, it would destroy its promising prospects. Success in keeping the Emergency Peace Service focused on principled law-enforcement will be reassuring, in particular, to many smaller and weaker states if they are confident that its aim will not be regime change or imposition of unwanted elements of globalization; moreover, principled enforcement will be reassuring to powerful states that their legitimate political interests will be respected by UNEPS.

The prospects for UNEPS to be established and to play a significant yet cautious role are enormously increased by the international community's recent acceptance of the idea that sovereignty carries responsibilities for every government to protect is own citizens from victimization by acts of genocide and crimes against humanity. Coupled to this idea of "sovereignty as responsibility" is endorsement of the norm that if a government is unable or unwilling to provide such protection, then the international community has a "responsibility to protect" people threatened with gross violations of their rights, even if it means coercive forms of intervention in a society to do so. This norm was reaffirmed in the United Nations Summit in 2005, which included the largest number of heads of government ever meeting together in world history. This understanding has been pointedly embraced by the UN Secretary-General who described the responsibility to protect as a "basis for collective action against genocide, ethnic cleansing and crimes against humanity. . . . If national authorities are unable or unwilling to protect their citizens, the responsibility then shifts to the international community." The Security Council "may take enforcement action. . . ."[6] Jan Eliasson, the President of the 60th General Assembly, described this norm as "one of the most important qualitative forward steps ever taken. . . ." It transforms the idea of sovereignty "from a defense mechanism into a test of accountability." If countries do not protect their own people, then "the international community has a responsibility to protect [them]. . . ."[7]

The UN's High-level Panel on Threats, Challenges and Change, in its recent report, *A More Secure World: Our Shared Responsibility*, emphasized the duty that the United Nations carries to address "violence within states," including "large-scale human rights abuses and genocide." [8] In particular, "when a State fails to protect its civilians, the international community then has a further responsibility to act, through humanitarian operations, monitoring missions and diplomatic pressure—and with force if necessary. . . ." Although the Panel noted that the Security Council "may well need to be prepared to be more proactive in the future, taking decisive action earlier," it stopped short of supplying the missing link in the implementation chain: the creation of a UN Emergency Service.[9]

Important though endorsement of the responsibility-to-protect norm truly is, it means nothing to potential victims who are threatened in their home communities unless the United Nations has an instrument to meet its responsibility to protect. Only an emergency service can meet this need.

To address a second major problem—that of ceasefire agreements in intra-state conflict breaking down and adversaries resuming violent conflict—both the High-level Panel and the Secretary-General, in his report *In Larger Freedom*, recommended the establishment of a Peacebuilding Commission, which the UN decided to establish in 2006. As the new Commission has taken shape, it becomes clear that the work of this Commission could be enormously aided by the existence of UNEPS, for example, if civilian law enforcement in a society emerging from violence needs to be bolstered immediately and impartially with external help. In addition, UNEPS could be deployed more wisely and effectively in cooperation with a Peacebuilding Commission that handled the design of programs to achieve conflict resolution in a war-torn society. UNEPS efforts to re-train indigenous civilian police and protect minority rights, for example, would be greatly enhanced by a larger set of programs aimed at reconciliation and economic integration within the society.[10] If "ethnic cleansing" threatened to recur in a tense situation, the Peacebuilding Commission would need to act quickly and with highest professionalism to avert it, and UNEPS could fulfill those requirements.

The intention of the Peacebuilding Commission to build local ownership of UN initiatives in war-torn societies and to work collaboratively with relevant non-governmental organizations would harmonize well with the goals of UNEPS to stop victimization. Recognizing and dealing with the possible tensions between military and civilian police enforcement in peace operations could increase the possibility that they could work well together to stop violence. Law enforcement, of course, is easier when a police mode of operations can arrest individuals engaging in misconduct than when a military mode of operations struggles to establish a ceasefire in the face of military aggression against a UN presence.

In another promising initiative, the United Nations is replacing the Human Rights Commission with a Human Rights Council. If a Human Rights Council is established as a principal organ within the UN system to help protect and promote human rights in all countries, and in particular to protect against gross violations, and if it is empowered to make recommendations on all such matters to the Security Council and General Assembly, it would need an enforcement instrument like UNEPS. Because the Council would have more legitimacy than the Commission has possessed, it could recommend immediate action by UNEPS in times of crisis. Such a recommendation could go either to the Security Council or, alternatively, in dire emergencies the Human Rights Council might directly deploy UNEPS, *if* it had previously been authorized by the Security Council or the General Assembly to do so. UNEPS could come quickly to the rescue of those threatened with loss of life or other crimes against humanity. When in the field, UNEPS could keep the Council informed with first-hand information, which could have been an important asset if a UNEPS presence had existed in the Darfur region of Sudan in 2004 or 2005.

Some participants pointed out that there could be a problem with authorizing UNEPS deployment too easily, perhaps in unwarranted situations in response to a national government's request for a UN intervention for narrowly self-serving reasons, such as to keep itself in power by attempting to use UN law enforcement to silence legitimate citizens' protests. UNEPS must be constructed in ways that people in civil societies will not fear that a UN intervention in their society would strengthen an existing government's efforts to oppress citizens seeking legitimate redress of grievances against a predatory government or other group. Of course UNEPS leadership could guard against this eventuality by emphasizing that its mandate is to uphold fundamental human rights by enforcing international humanitarian and human rights law, rather than upholding a particular government. But this line may not be easy to draw in some cases. It also is important to have developed and publicized ways to discourage people from instigating violence deliberately in the hope of triggering UNEPS intervention.

Can UNEPS Succeed Without the Consent of the State Where It Is Deployed?

All participants agreed that it is necessary to clarify the differences between coercive and consensual deployments of UNEPS. Whenever consent is present or can be arranged, all aspects of the operation become easier, from initial authorization to effectiveness of operations in the field. Simply the existence of a permanent UN Emergency Peace Service is likely to elicit consent in some cases where consent might otherwise not have been forthcoming in the absence of an immediately-available, non-partisan UNEPS. When a government is subjected to coercive (Chapter VII) deployment, UNEPS should continually strive to elicit informal consent for an operation, especially among the local population, while doing law enforcement in a manner that serves citizens' needs for law and domestic tranquility.

Any Chapter VII deployment means facing direct combat, participants emphasized, but it should be a form of combat that is different from combat in most wars. Its purpose is law enforcement and protection of innocent people, not territorial conquest or to vanquish a foe. UNEPS should aim to move as quickly as possible from combat to a police mode of enforcement. Combat should be limited to the last reasonable resort and be guided by human rights goals. UNEPS must always strictly follow international humanitarian law in an exemplary fashion. Interventions must do more good than harm.

Skeptics expressed reservations about whether UNEPS should be deployed in contexts where the host refuses to give consent—unless the United Nations first developed a much larger UN military capability and its own strategic command structure. However, the prevailing view was that, in carefully selected contexts, where large-scale war-fighting is not necessary, the proposed UNEPS could successfully dampen the conflict and save the lives of many people. To be sure, an improved UN strategic command capability is essential for UNEPS to succeed, but this would be far more feasible than to develop a full-fledged strategic military command structure anticipated in the days when Article 43 agreements and a fully functioning Military Staff Committee were considered realistic possibilities. Most participants felt that the proposed UNEPS provides an attractive—even essential—upgrade in UN capability while shifting focus away from the UN's inability to fight large wars and toward the virtue of empowering it to enforce law against genocide.

Participants also stressed that many UNEPS deployments would probably occur with the consent of the host state and thereby be spared the problems of a Chapter VII framework. The substantial utility of UNEPS in consensual deployments *alone* would justify the creation of the Emergency Peace Service.

Who Should Authorize Deployment?

What Role Should the Secretary-General Play?

All participants agreed that the Security Council is the preferred body for authorizing UNEPS. However, in event that the Security Council is prevented from acting by a veto, what should happen? Most agreed that the UN General Assembly might also authorize UNEPS deployment by following procedures like those in the Uniting for Peace Resolution (1950). The group also discussed the possibility of authorizing the Secretary-General to deploy the UN Emergency Peace Service if the necessary conditions, specified in advance by the Security Council, had, in the Secretary-General's judgment, been met. The Security Council could still withdraw the force if it determined that the Secretary-General had made a mistake. Although some thought that recommending an authorizing role for the Secretary-General would undermine support for UNEPS, it seems to this rapporteur that many of the substantive arguments against pre-authorization of deployment by the Secretary-General are unconvincing. The idea might become politically more acceptable if it would be better understood. On the one hand, if an emergency arose in which the Secretary-General decided to deploy UNEPS to stop genocide, he or she would be unlikely to depart from pre-existing guidelines because of the negative political ramifications and the prospect of a Security Council reversal of the decision if the Secretary-General abused his or her authority. On the other hand, if the Secretary-General would prove to be reluctant to intervene, no deployment would occur, producing the same outcome as would occur with a Security Council unable to pass a resolution.

Of course heavy emphasis should be placed on the Permanent Members' moral obligation to heed two relevant recommendations of the High-level Panel on Threats, Challenges and Change, namely, that the veto should "be limited to matters where vital interests are genuinely at stake" and that the Permanent Members should "pledge themselves to refrain from the use of the veto in cases of genocide and large-scale human rights abuses."[11] If this compelling request is honored, the question of authorization by the Secretary-General would not arise.

Perhaps the question of Secretary-General authorization could be presented as a tradeoff between (1) a Security Council commitment to refrain from vetoing resolutions to protect people from gross violations of human rights[12] and (2) a Security Council commitment to authorize the Secretary-General to act if the Council would be prevented from doing so by the veto. If the Permanent Members would promise not to veto resolutions by following the suggested guidelines of the High-level Panel, then even pre-approval of Secretary-General authorization would not be likely to result in a Secretary-General's decision to deploy. But having that option available would help keep the Council honest. In turn, the ability of the Council to reverse the Secretary-General would help to keep the Secretary-General honest. If the Security Council in some cases would fail to pass a resolution for deployment because it lacked a majority in favor, rather than because of a veto of a majority vote, it would be unwise, and should be specified as unacceptable, for the Secretary-General to deploy UNEPS in such circumstances.

In any case, if carefully constructed, a Security Council-authorized provision for conditional Secretary-General authorization to deploy UNEPS when an extreme emergency arises, in which a veto prevents passage of a resolution that is favored by at least 9 members of the Security Council, may sufficiently address concerns about potential abuse that this provision can be retained in the proposal. The likelihood that many lives might be saved with prompt deployment probably outweighs the likelihood that a Secretary-General would abuse this authority.

What Role Should Regional Organizations Play in Authorizing Deployment?

Significant divergence of views existed at the experts meeting in Cuenca on the possible relationship of regional organizations to UNEPS. Over the past decade there has been a dramatic rise in peace operations assigned to or seized by regional organizations or a regional hegemon acting within a legitimizing regional organization. In fact, most recent peace operations involve regional organizations in one way or another. This rising role for regional actors is due to their increasing interest because subregional conflicts often affect an entire region. In addition, there is a rising norm that states have a responsibility to address the problem of weak or failing states, in part because of the responsibility to protect people from victimization. A third factor is the inability of the UN to deal with regional crises because it has no effective rapid reaction capability. Primacy for a UN role has diminished so far that a UN mandate is no longer considered necessary by some actors before they intervene. The NATO bombing of Serbs in Kosovo is an example. Some participants noted that regionalism may be rising not because it is "natural," but instead because U.S. opposition to multilateralism and collective decision-making at the United Nations has pushed the need for response to the regional level.

Some manifestations of regionalism may undermine efforts to uphold norms of peace because regionalism can fragment the stabilizing monopoly of the UN on authorizing the legitimate use of military force in all cases except legitimate acts of self-defense. To depart from that monopoly could allow the abuse of power by regional hegemons and regional organizations acting collectively. As a result, many participants did not think that the possibility of interventionary force authorized by regional organizations would be a positive development. Cynical regional departures from global norms obviously can detract from the universal human rights principles that should undergird UNEPS. Most participants preferred to provide the UN with the capability needed for it to maintain a monopoly on the right to authorize the interventionary use of force. Of course for consensual deployments this issue of regional vs. UN authorization does not arise as sharply, but even in consensual cases there still could be differences between regional and Security Council justifications for sending UNEPS into particular circumstances.

Several participants voiced strong objections to allowing UNEPS to operate outside the context of UN authorization, pointing out the dangers of inter-regional differences and of lost legitimacy when a less than universal organization might try to employ UNEPS. Others noted the need to protect weaker societies from being threatened by regional hegemons, suggesting it might be politically wiser for UNEPS to be employed only with UN authorization. Of course it is possible to strengthen regional and global cooperation at the same time while still retaining a UN monopoly on the right to authorize interventionary use of force, particularly if the UN could make expeditious decisions and the permanent members discouraged each other from using the veto to obstruct resolutions designed to stop gross violations of human rights.

A possible compromise might be to allow UNEPS authorization by clearly designated regional organizations in special cases when a majority of the Security Council favors UNEPS deployment but is prevented from authorizing it because of a veto by one or two permanent members. This approach would, at the least, ensure a UN authorizing role and widespread support for UNEPS deployment, but it would not prevent UNEPS deployment by one or two permanent members who resisted a Council majority vote for narrowly self-interested reasons. Regional and global co-authorization could work well, although controversies over the administration and financing of the intervention could still arise. Of course regional organizations could help promote and educate people about the values of UNEPS.

Is UNEPS Needed in Addition to Other Rapid-reaction Initiatives?

Concerned governments have been working for years to establish a rapid-reaction capacity for the UN, as illustrated by the Multinational Standby High Readiness Brigade for UN Peace Operations, the UN Standby Arrangements System, and the Standby High Readiness Police Battalion for UN Operations. Yet these initiatives are standby arrangements that still require last-minute approval of individual governments and are not immediately ready to enter the field. There are at least six reasons why UNEPS is still needed, in addition to other helpful initiatives by the United Nations and regional organizations, none of which will be displaced by UNEPS:

1. As a permanent, dedicated service, UNEPS could be deployed on 24-48 hours notice. No other existing agencies can.

2. A permanent, dedicated service can have better trained and more carefully selected personnel who possess a combination of interlocking skills that are needed for this kind of protective mission.

3. An individually selected service, drawn carefully from highly qualified volunteers, can make it easier for governments in the Security Council to decide to deploy it because they are not deploying their own (or any other) national units.

4. A permanent, dedicated service can be more skillfully commanded because it is totally integrated, has always trained in a unified command structure, and has no conflicting national commitments.

5. A permanent, truly cosmopolitan law enforcement service

is more likely to be, and to be perceived to be, free of national partisanship than multinational groups made up of nationally contributed contingents.

6.   A permanent, highly professionalized service could establish a long-standing reputation of impartiality with procedures to prevent abuse of enforcement powers toward local inhabitants and more credible, transparent grievance processes to address any misdeeds by UNEPS personnel if they should arise.

How Can UNEPS Ensure Respect for Women's Human Rights?

In creating an exemplary form of international law enforcement, attention needs to be given to full representation of women in all aspects of planning, management, hiring, command, and decision-making, as well as to realize their rights, equal status, and fair treatment in the field. In implementing UN resolution 1325, [13] which calls for mainstreaming gender sensitivity, it is necessary but insufficient to include women in all parts of UNEPS operations; gender training for men is also necessary to assure the effective functioning of UNEPS and its appropriate enforcement of law in the field.

Natural Disasters and Environmental Accidents

Most participants support UNEPS authorization to address natural or environmental disasters, but only when these threaten large-scale loss of life and are not being addressed by other agencies or governments. Such a deployment would usually not be a coercive intervention; however, if massive loss of life were threatened in a case where consent for deployment was not forthcoming, then properly authorized coercive deployment would be acceptable.

Specific Issues

Recruiting Individuals and Avoiding Bureaucratic Ineptitude

Although one participant recommended that personnel for UNEPS be deputized or succunded from national forces and rotated out of UNEPS on a fixed 3-year basis so as to avoid becoming mired in bureaucratic problems of recruitment and appointment in UN agencies, a preponderance of experts valued the coherence, unity, and beneficial professionalization that would arise from direct UN recruitment and careful selection of individuals from among those who would volunteer to work in the UN Emergency Peace Service. Selection and terms of service should be based on the highest professional criteria, not subject to political manipulation, and able to root out dead wood or internal corruption if it occurs.

Ensuring Lawful Conduct When Enforcing the Law

The UNEPS proposal should state directly the absolute obligation to conduct exemplary operations in accord with international human rights and humanitarian law. A high degree of transparency, an ombudsperson, and grievance procedures for injured parties are essential. Where legal issues arise, related either to authorization or operations, they should be referred to the International Criminal Court, the International Court of Justice, or to other relevant tribunals that exist or might be created, depending on the nature of the legal question.

Ensuring a Backup for UNEPS

UNEPS will complement—not replace—other UN or regional agencies and stand-by services for peace operations and in some cases will need to rely on them after an initial deployment. They should be prepared to come to the aid of UNEPS if unexpected difficulties put the success of its mission in jeopardy.

Ensuring Mobility

Further study is required of whether the UN should acquire its own air transport capabilities for UNEPS or instead obtain standing agreements with several UN members or regional organizations to provide air transport when needed.

Considering Phased Implementation

If the most contested element of UNEPS is its permanent military capability, then should UNEPS be implemented in a first phase without that robust enforcement element? In considering a phased implementation in which the least controversial dimensions—the humanitarian assistance, civilian police, judicial and conflict resolution functions—might be established without the armed security service, most participants emphasized that to be effective the entire proposal must be kept in an inseparable package. Although a phased implementation of different components might increase the political feasibility of establishing a severely limited emergency service relatively quickly, it would not provide the comprehensive services—especially robust security—needed to meet the demands likely to be placed on an interventionary service in difficult humanitarian crises.

Agreeing on General Principles

The diverse views expressed in discussing proposals have added great strength to the development of UNEPS. After exhaustive discussions of major issues, strong agreement exists on the following principles:

1.　The international community urgently needs a United Nations Emergency Peace Service capable of responding promptly to genocide, war crimes, and crimes against humanity that are not being addressed by other responsible parties. Even the most critical comments primarily emphasized the difficulties for UNEPS; they did not reduce the expressed *need* for UNEPS. No other agency can do what needs to be done.

2.　UNEPS would be obligated to operate within and to enforce international humanitarian and human rights law.

3.　UNEPS should be permanent and highly mobile.

4.　It should be composed of individuals selected from among those who would volunteer, reflecting the diversity of all major cultural regions of the world, with the goal of equitable representation of women and men.

5.　The members of UNEPS should be carefully screened and highly trained.

6.　UNEPS should include people with a diversity of professional and language skills covering these areas: human rights, gender, civilian police, military service, humanitarian assistance, judicial proceedings and penal matters, conflict transformation, and environmental protection.

7.　UNEPS should function within a unified command under UN authority.

8.   UNEPS should include up to 15 thousand personnel at the outset.

9.   UNEPS should be financed through the regular UN budget.

10. The preferred procedure for authorizing use of UNEPS would be action by the Security Council.

11. UNEPS also could be authorized for use by the General Assembly, following processes similar to those used under Uniting for Peace procedures, when the Security Council is prevented from taking action because of the veto power of the Permanent Members.

12. Women's human rights should be upheld and a thoroughgoing gender perspective should be fully integrated, as detailed in UN Resolution 1325, in all aspects of UNEPS' organization and operations.

13. UNEPS could address humanitarian crises caused by natural disasters or environmental accidents if other national governments or intergovernmental organizations or relevant humanitarian agencies were unable or unwilling to avert major loss of human life.

14. UNEPS would produce important benefits once established. It could deter, prevent, or stop genocide and crimes against humanity in many contexts, although of course not in all.

Four points of reassurance need emphasis:

1.   Everyone anticipates political difficulties in establishing UNEPS; no one can know how or when they will be overcome. The important point is to develop a proposal in which North and South can find common ground so that when the time is right—perhaps triggered by one or more crises—implementation will be possible. It is reassuring to recall that no one thought the international community would be able to establish an International Criminal Court like the one we now have—even a half dozen years before the treaty was finalized at Rome in 1998.

2.   UNEPS does not solve all problems. Even though it can not address every crisis, for critics to identify a situation that UNEPS could not handle is not in itself a convincing argument against UNEPS. Our claim is simply that the world would be better off

with UNEPS than without it—economically, militarily, politically, and ethically. That claim can be convincingly substantiated.

3.   UNEPS will not replace any existing regional or UN security arrangements; it would complement them and often work in tandem with them.

4.   UNEPS should be an exemplary agency in every way—in providing law enforcement without abuse of police or military power; in being gender sensitive in the composition, action, and leadership of the service; in training personnel with high professionalism; and in honoring international law in its operations and practices.

Topics Requiring Further Analysis

On the following questions, where opinion is divided, further study is necessary:

1.   What are the benefits and costs of proposing that the decision to deploy UNEPS could be authorized by the Secretary-General under emergency conditions specified in advance by the Security Council for justifiable use of the Service?

2.   How can regional security organizations and a UN Emergency Peace Service be best shaped to help each other? What should be the role of regional organizations in enforcing law against genocide, war crimes, and crimes against humanity? If regional forces are to be used to protect people threatened in a humanitarian crisis, should they be authorized by the UN, as a general rule, to maintain a UN monopoly on the authorization of interventionary force? Might a regional force legitimately intervene without Security Council authorization? Should UNEPS be deployed as a result of authorization by a regional intergovernmental organization, following its normal multilateral decision-making procedures, in the territory of one of the members of the regional organization? Or, in the absence of a clear Security Council authorization for UNEPS deployment due to a veto, might UNEPS nonetheless be deployed with what might be considered a "co-authorization," comprised of both (1) an affirmative decision for deployment by a regional organization and (2) an affirmative vote by a majority

of Security Council members but without the passage of a deployment resolution because of a veto by a permanent member?

3.   Should UNEPS be deployed in some circumstances for the purpose of preventing armed conflict as well as for preventing violations of laws prohibiting genocide, crimes against humanity, and war crimes?

4.   How can the management and functioning of UNEPS be shaped to reassure the Global South that an interventionary capability will advance their legitimate interests rather than undermine them? Can there be some form of review, judicial or otherwise, to protect recipients of intervention against injury and unwarranted political intrusion?

5.   What should be the principles guiding the withdrawal of UNEPS once it is deployed? One condition should be a reasonable expectation that the threats that brought UNEPS into a country in the first place will not be repeated. Can this condition or others be specified more precisely to give credence to UNEPS' purpose of enforcing law against heinous crimes, rather than pursuing other political purposes?

6.   How will UNEPS deal with tensions between the military and the nonmilitary aspects of its role? Often nonmilitary personnel (such as for humanitarian assistance) gain acceptance in local settings by not working hand-in-glove with military personnel. How would the dynamic work with UNEPS? What can be done to emphasize that providing security with military personnel will not simply be military combat as traditionally understood? Nonmilitary personnel might be more readily invited to enter a society than military personnel. If a UNEPS deployment is consensual but the host government explicitly does not want any military units to be sent, how should UNEPS respond?

7.   How can advocates of UNEPS think more creatively about responding to the worldwide tendency to under-emphasize nonmilitary security measures and to overemphasize the militarization of security issues?

8.   Should UNEPS address non-state actors engaging in crimes against humanity, such as transnational networks conducting

terrorist activities? If so, what guidelines would apply?

9.   How would UNEPS gather early warning signals about imminent threats? Prompt action by UNEPS to prevent crises is more desirable than subsequent warnings of imminent or actual bloodshed. How can the UN develop effective procedures for handling information to prompt early antidotes to crimes against humanity?.

10. How would UNEPS relate to other UN offices and agencies, such as the Special Adviser to the Secretary-General on the Prevention of Genocide (who could provide early-warning information), the Department of Political Affairs, the Department of Peacekeeping Operations, the UN Peacebuilding Commission, the UN Development Program, the UN Development Fund for Women, the UN High Commissioner for Human Rights, the UN High Commissioner for Refugees, and other relevant agencies?

11. More clarity is needed on how to apply the international laws governing the use of force. UNEPS should not be part of expanding national uses of armed force, but instead should expand the enforcement of laws constricting the abuse of force against innocent people. What changes in international law would UNEPS facilitate or necessitate? More clarity is needed, for example, on the differences between the legitimate use of force to stop war crimes, genocide, and crimes against humanity, on the one hand, and all other uses of armed force.

12. What is the preferred relationship between UNEPS and the International Criminal Court? Should UNEPS arrest people who have been indicted by the Court? Of course context matters. If UNEPS had been deployed in Darfur and came across some of the 51 persons named by the UN Commission of Inquiry, presumably they should be apprehended. On the other hand, it would be unwise to precipitate war in order to make arrests.

13. Is a treaty required, or could some other procedure be used to establish UNEPS? How can efforts to establish UNEPS be informed by the successful coalition of non-governmental organizations, UN agencies, and governments that created the International Criminal Court? How many countries would need to support the idea before it could become reality? How much attention should be focused

on medium or small powers? Great powers? Members of national parliaments? Civil society organizations? Journalists?

Developing an Effective Strategy

Participants at the Cuenca meetings noted that some current political realities are signs of promise for UNEPS, while other realities represent problems to be overcome. Regardless, the following political considerations should inform the strategy for establishing a UN Emergency Peace Service:

1. Governments in the Global South are understandably skeptical of an instrument that might be used to intervene forcefully in their societies. Fears of neo-imperialism need to be addressed by strict guidelines on the nature and possibly the duration of UNEPS' operations. Will UNEPS conduct any long-term peacebuilding missions, or instead limit itself to a "first in, first out" Emergency Peace Service not to be deployed for more than 6 months?[14] How will it relate to longer-term peacebuilding activities and agencies, such as the Peacebuilding Commission and UN Development Program?

People living in a society where they fear victimization by their own government may be more welcoming to UNEPS than their government, especially if the government or powerful groups within that society could be deterred by UNEPS from ruthless, illegal conduct. UNEPS can serve, its advocates should explain, the legitimate interests of people within a country even if their government is unwelcoming. In any case, continuing conversations with governments and civil societies in the South are essential for addressing concerns and clarifying that UNEPS operations are fundamentally different from the U.S. invasion of Iraq in 2003 to change the Iraqi government. Some support for UNEPS exists in the Global South because of its potential to be a stabilizing, life-saving, cost-averting presence.

2. The most powerful industrialized states are skeptical about creating UNEPS because they often do not want the United Nations to be a much more capable institution. Nonetheless, UNEPS can serve their interests in stopping mass murder and population displacement, as well as reducing the costs of hu-

manitarian assistance after bloodshed that is likely if UNEPS is not created. Support for UNEPS exists in the North among some governments that have for years favored enhancing UN rapid reaction capability. UNEPS would also complement several European governments' emphasis on cooperation between civil society and intergovernmental agencies in humanitarian work. In another initiative, taken in cooperation with other governments, Germany has organized a "friends of conflict prevention" group that could be engaged conceptually with UNEPS and also could ask the Security Council to hold discussions on genocide prevention. Norway, Germany, and other countries are now training civilian police with an eye to assisting international needs for such personnel, which could help pave the way and complement any plans for establishing UNEPS.

3.   As suggested in the preceding two points, arguments for UNEPS that appeal to the long-term economic and political self-interest of national governments—in both the South and North—can be used in combination with legal and moral arguments to build broad political support.

4.   Encouraging more conversation among influential governments in the South, such as India, Brazil, South Africa and others, about the "responsibility to protect" and the prospects for UNEPS is essential for building necessary political support.

5.   The credibility of UNEPS will be influenced by whether there is genuine movement to strengthen the rule of law in world affairs more generally. If so, UNEPS enforcement will be viewed positively. If not, it will be seen as an instrument carrying out a set of double standards where big powers use coercive means against weaker societies. If international law is not upheld in a balanced and reciprocal way, UNEPS can hardly be established, or if established, cannot blossom forth.

6.   Numerous participants pointed out that it is important to emphasize the role of UNEPS in *preventing* crimes, rather than focus primarily on its ability to fight pitched battles in chaotic situations after fighting has occurred. If UNEPS could be immediately available and effective, in some instances it would not need to be brought in because its availability would deter po-

tential law-breakers from laying plans that would trigger international intervention. Special Adviser to the Secretary-General on the Prevention of Genocide, Juan Mendez, emphasized in the Cuenca meetings that establishment of UNEPS is a natural follow-on to his mandate to inform the Secretary-General about the threat of genocide before it erupts. If the UN is to address such threats effectively, rapid response with effective law enforcement is required. The UN needs more numerous and effectively trained civilian police because they cannot be obtained in adequate numbers from UN members. If UNEPS had existed, it would probably have helped deter crimes in Darfur in 2004. Although political will is often lacking in Security Council deliberations, it could be strengthened if an enforcement instrument were immediately available for the Council to deploy. Mendez emphasized that his job could be carried out more effectively if UNEPS existed.

7. The civilian police and humanitarian dimensions of UNEPS should be highlighted so people do not focus primarily on the military dimension. The consensual uses of UNEPS, in which the host state would invite a UNEPS presence, should be elaborated, while also spelling out the need for coercive enforcement. The proposal should note that international law does not allow wide latitude for coercive enforcement, thereby reassuring those concerned about too much latitude for humanitarian intervention.

8. To minimize the negative consequences of political conflicts that sometimes arise among UN or regional agencies over how to proceed with new initiatives, UNEPS supporters encourage dialogue with all relevant agencies, from the Department of Peacekeeping Operations to the UN High Commissioner for Refugees, and from the UN High Commissioner for Human Rights to the United Nations Development Program. UNEPS should be gracefully connected, to the extent possible, to relevant UN reform recommendations from the Secretary-General, the High-level Panel on Threats, Challenges, and Change, and the International Commission of Inquiry on Darfur. UNEPS should also be related to other relevant initiatives, such as Under Secretary-General for Peacekeeping Jean-Marie Guehenno's interest in a UN strategic reserve and his call for a standing civilian police capability. The UNEPS campaign should

be in conversation with state-based efforts, such as in Norway and Germany, to train civilian police in ways that could enable them to be well prepared for international duty in genocide prevention, as a complement or backup to UNEPS.

The preceding initiatives demonstrate the utility of UNEPS. When the High-level Panel concluded that "prompt and effective response to today's challenges requires a dependable capacity for the rapid deployment of personnel and equipment for peacekeeping and law enforcement," it seems clear that UNEPS could meet the requirement. When the Secretary-General recommended more principled UN oversight to ensure that enforcement operations are in accord with international law and called for a Rule of Law Assistance Unit in the proposed Peacebuilding Support Office,[15] UNEPS could dovetail smoothly with this initiative to help strengthen international practices in law enforcement.

9. An important benefit of the Working Group description of a UN Emergency Peace Service is that it provides governments and NGOs with a single proposal on which to focus analysis, debate, and action. This was needed but did not exist when, in the early 1990s, both the U.S. and French presidents said, along with a few other heads of government, that the world should have a UN rapid-deployment force. In part because of the absence of a single, well-developed proposal and concerted political effort on its behalf, an opportunity was lost, costing years of delay and hundreds of thousands of lives. Building widespread support for the set of principles (in the section "Agreeing on General Principles" above) is a key to progress. UNEPS' attractiveness springs in part from its ability to provide a flexible yet comprehensive set of services in a single agency by highly trained individuals working together within a coherent plan legitimized through worldwide support. It recognizes that one enforcement size will never fit all humanitarian crises.

10. Participants identified the need for further research and more detailed analyses and blueprints[16] to supplement the current proposal with additional materials, including a comprehensive list of frequently asked questions and expert answers.

In addition, a series of case studies, drawn from concrete examples of successful UN peace operations (e.g., East Timor) or UN failures due to inaction (e.g., Rwanda), would be useful to show how a permanent Emergency Peace Service could have improved upon the results of *ad hoc* UN arrangements and the failure to act at all.

11. To formulate more clearly the conceptual differences between armed security operations for law enforcement by UNEPS and conventional military combat for vanquishing an enemy can help to expand support in general and cooperation in particular between peace groups and human rights organizations. These groups have been estranged somewhat on issues such as military intervention to protect human rights as occurred with high altitude aerial bombardment to stop ethnic "cleansing" in Kosovo. Thoughtful presentation of UNEPS' uses of power will also help to narrow the gap between military organizations and human rights groups by expanding common ground for implementing security and human rights goals.

12. If some national governments in the South are predatory in relating to their own populations and others in the North are calloused in accepting predatory consequences of globalization or forms of globalization that cause a global democratic deficit for millions of people, it is useful to emphasize that UNEPS is an initiative that civil society organizations and progressive governments can spearhead to reduce negative consequences of predatory conduct in both domains, by upholding some fundamental human rights.

13. In developing a strategy to establish UNEPS, we should draw upon recent experiences of successful transnational political processes, particularly the effort to draft a statute for the International Criminal Court.[17] Civil society organizations have been a powerful ingredient in recent successes. Because the present UNEPS proposal is focused mainly on states, another statement is needed to highlight NGOs interests in UNEPS. The network for the International Criminal Court drew strength from a broad coalition that agreed on key principles for an independent court, despite differing organizational emphases, and from the moral

high ground that the campaign enjoyed because it sought to end impunity for heinous crimes, maintained high international legitimacy and technical credibility, and expanded all actors' accountability. A UNEPS campaign could bring parallel strengths to the political process because UNEPS can protect innocent people in accord with humanity's highest moral and legal commitments.

14. Political opposition needs to be addressed seriously, but it should not be allowed to discourage proponents of UNEPS. The UN Secretary-General may not advocate UNEPS explicitly at this time, for example, but he is not likely to oppose it. He may think it does not now have the support it needs. To take another example, the world should not wait for all permanent members of the Security Council to endorse the idea before taking serious steps to establish UNEPS. The day is likely to come, at a time we cannot predict, when views will change. Our responsibility is to develop the best possible proposal, build international support for it, and push it toward establishment when global political and moral forces enable these preparations to bear fruit.

Endorsing the United Nations Emergency Peace Service

To help protect innocent people against horrible victimization yet again, the creation of UNEPS needs to proceed with an implementation strategy that focuses simultaneously on: international discussions to ensure worldwide shaping and ownership of the proposal, education to increase people's understanding of UNEPS' promise, research to ensure that UNEPS will be effective, and political action to build a transnational, influential coalition for establishing UNEPS. Individuals and organizations can advance the cause by discussing the proposal with their own constituents and obtaining agreement in principle with the UNEPS proposal.

Endnotes

[1]The meeting was co-hosted by Global Action to Prevent War, the Center for Peace Research in Madrid, and the faculty of social sciences at the University of Castilla–La Mancha. The meeting was made possible by a generous grant from the Ford Foundation and vital financial support from the Global Legal Studies Program of Rutgers University School of Law.

[2]Of course if deployment is not a coercive or Chapter VII intervention because the host government has consented to a UNEPS presence, then the fourth criterion would not apply or delay deployment.

[3]International Commission on Intervention and State Sovereignty, *The Responsibility to Protect: Report* (Ottawa, Canada: International Development Research Centre, 2001), 20. See also Carnegie Commission on Preventing Deadly Conflict, *The Costs of Conflict: Prevention and Cure in the Global Arena* eds. Michael E. Brown and Richard N. Rosecrance (Lanham, Md: Rowman & Littlefield, 1999).

[4]Secretary-General Kofi Annan, "Secretary-General's Annual Report to the General Assembly," *UN Press Release*, 20 September 1999: 5.

[5]Kofi Annan, "Two Concepts of Sovereignty," *The Economist*, 18 September 1999, 49. Emphasis added.

[6]UN Secretary-General Kofi Annan, *In Larger Freedom: Towards Development, Security, and Human Rights for All*, United Nations General Assembly, A/59/2005, 2005, 4.

[7]Barbara Crossette, "Year in Review: Moving Forward," *The Interdependent* 3, no. 4 (2005/06).

[8](New York: United Nations, 2004), 2.

[9]Ibid., 4-5. The Panel did note a strong need for more stand-by forces. Some participants reported, off the record, that they did discuss the need for a rapid response capability, but dropped the idea of recommending the creation of it when the some said that it would not be politically feasible given U.S. reluctance to strengthen international law enforcement.

[10]The Peacebuilding Commission is likely to have goals that would parallel and reinforce the work of UNEPS, such as "to establish the trust of the local population from the outset of a field operation . . . ," and "to foster conditions for long-term local dialogue, compromise, consensus-building, and conflict resolution as the only viable path towards a just and durable peace." Richard Ponzio, "The Creation and Function-

ing of the UN Peacebuilding Commission," *Saferworld* (2005): 5-6.

[11]High-level Panel on Threats, Challenges, and Change, *A More Secure World: Our Shared Responsibility* (New York: United Nations, 2004), A/59/565, para. 256.

[12]Of course nine affirmative votes would still be required for passage of a resolution. A permanent member could vote against a resolution without the vote counting as a veto if less than 9 votes were cast in favor of the resolution.

[13]United Nations S/RES/1325 (2000), 31 October 2000.

[14]Logistical problems could arise if UNEPS attempted a deployment lasting for more than a half year.

[15]UN Secretary-General Kofi Annan, "In Larger Freedom: Towards Development, Security, and Human Rights for All" (New York: United Nations General Assembly A/59/2005), Report Paragraph 137; available at http://www.un.org/largerfreedom/contents.htm, accessed 7 April 2005.

[16]These could build upon H. Peter Langille, *Bridging the Commitment-Capacity Gap: A Review of Existing Arrangements and Options for Enhancing UN Rapid Deployment* (Wayne, NJ: Center for UN Reform Education, 2002); and Saul Mendlovitz and John Fousek, "A UN Constabulary to Enforce the Law on Genocide and Crimes Against Humanity," in Neil Reimer (ed.), *Protection Against Genocide: Mission Impossible?* (London: Praeger, 2000), 105-22.

[17]See also H. Peter Langille, "Building a Global Constituency for a UN Emergency Service," unpublished paper distributed to conference participants, 27 April 2004.

4

AFTERWORD

Lieutenant General Satish Nambiar

The report on the workshop discussions held at Cuenca, Spain in February 2005, so painstakingly compiled by Robert Johansen, is indeed a comprehensive and accurate account of our deliberations. The report reflects the unanimous agreement amongst all participants that an effective UN rapid reaction capability is essential if the international community is to be able to deal promptly and effectively with situations of genocide and crimes against humanity. At the workshop, I had expressed my disappointment that the United Nations Secretary-General's High Level Panel that I had the privilege of serving on did not consider it appropriate to recommend the setting up of a Standing United Nations Rapid Deployment Force as I had suggested. I have been a strong advocate of such a force for almost a decade now. Therefore, I consider it a privilege to be associated with the proposal to establish a United Nations Emergency Peace Service (UNEPS).

The proposal comes at an appropriate moment in the evolution of changes in the international system set in motion by the Outcome Document adopted at the World Summit, held at the United Nations Headquarters in New York from 14 to 16 September 2005. Notwithstanding its other inadequacies in shying away from what could have been radical and bold steps that were indeed called for, the Outcome Document endorses the recommendations of the United Nations Secretary-General on the "responsibility to protect populations from genocide, war crimes, ethnic cleansing and crimes against humanity." To that extent, there is already high-level formal UN endorsement of the basis for the UNEPS proposal described in this volume. Threshold criteria for such intervention are documented in the report of the High Level Panel as endorsed by the United Nations Secretary-General. The culpability of the international community in some of the events of the last decade or so cannot be glossed over. However, while stressing that early deployment of United Nations forces could have prevented or minimized the excesses that took place, it would be naïve in the extreme to ignore that much of what transpired was due not only to the non-availability of forces but even more to the unwillingness to act expediently through sheer lack of understanding of the consequences.

I cannot forego this opportunity to briefly express views on some aspects of the UNEPS proposal that I feel need detailed consideration or review as we move ahead. First, regarding deployment of a UNEPS force, I feel it should only be done under the authority of the Security Council or the General Assembly. I do not think such authority should be delegated either to the Secretary-General or to a regional organization. This does not detract from regional organizations deploying capability created wholly within those respective regions. Given my recommendation, it is important for an organ like the Security Council to be made more representative and democratic. I have no doubt we will discuss this further. Second, I have severe reservations about deploying a United Nations force under Chapter VII provisions that might involve direct combat. This is primarily because the United Nations as structured today is not in a position to provide strategic direction so essential in the conduct of combat operations where we are dealing with the lives of people, both from the UN force as well as from local adversarial elements.

Third, I have some reservations about the recruitment pattern suggested in the report. Given the little experience I have with the working of the United Nations staff, and that from a field commander's point of view, I fear that if there is a permanent structure imposed on the components of UNEPS, including recruitment, performance will in due course degenerate into a bureaucratic mould lacking responsibility and accountability. We may be left with a bunch of "Gladiators." On the other hand, recruits from member states selected from among qualified volunteers to perform for a specified period of three years or so will return to their home countries and be of use both in assisting in the training of local expertise, and in spreading the good word about UNEPS. Fourth, given the fact that action has been initiated for setting up a United Nations Peacebuilding Commission and support infrastructure, it would be best that the UNEPS does not assume this responsibility. And finally, allow me to suggest that when advocating assistance in setting up "rule of law" mechanisms to address failed/failing state scenarios, we not only look to developed countries, but also draw on the expertise available in many developing countries that have established mechanisms for conduct of elections, the civilian police, the judiciary, and so on.

I have no doubt the UNEPS initiative will receive full endorsement and support, becoming a reality in the not too distant future. I look forward to continued association with the initiative.

5

COMMENTS

UNEPS: AN AFRICAN PERSPECTIVE

Hussein Solomon

That Africa is wracked by conflict is self-evident. In North Africa, the decades-long low intensity conflict between Morocco and the Polisario Front continues. Egypt's election of 2005 was plagued with violence and, in Algeria, the terrorist threat posed by the violent Salafist Group for Preaching and Combat remains unfortunately all too real. Gaddafi's Tripoli also confronts Islamic militants in the form of the Fighting Islamic Group (FIG) and the Islamic Matyrdom Brigades.

In the Horn of Africa, the Darfur region of Sudan continues to generate death, refugees, and victims of rape as the government-backed Janjaweed militias and the rebel-led Sudan Liberation Army (SLA) and Justice and Equality Movement (JEM) continue their macabre dance of death. Somalia continues to be without a functioning government as various warlords fight each other in an effort to enlarge their respective fiefdoms. Tensions have escalated between Ethiopia and Eritrea as each engages in military manoeuvres along their common border to press their competing claims of territory. In West Africa, whilst Liberians have elected Ellen Johnson-Sirleaf as their president and hope that this would usher in a period of peace, there are still others who refuse to accept her authority. In the Ivory Coast, there is hope that the civil war would come to an end with the appointment of an interim Prime Minister. However, this peace is extremely fragile as various political factions demand increasingly more unrealistic concessions for participation in an election process. And what of the regional superpower—Nigeria? This country is wracked by ethnic conflict in the Delta region pitting Ijaws against Itsekeris. In addition, various other ethnic groupings have established their own militant operations in recent years such as the Oodua People's Congress (OPC).

In East Africa, political tensions between the Kenyan government and the opposition regarding proposed changes to the national constitution have turned violent. With government increasingly less inclined to dialogue and more willing to deploy its security apparatus, Nairobi is on a violent trajectory. In Uganda, the areas of Gulu and Kitgum in the north continue to mean death and despair for the Acholi people as government forces engage with the Lords Resistance Army (LRA) rebels. The rebels intend to overthrow the secular government of Yoweri Museveni and to replace it with one that conforms to the biblical Ten Commandments. Ironically, in the course of this resistance, the commandment "Thou Shall Not Kill" has been violated thousands of times.

In Central Africa, conflict continues to plague the two Congos. In Congo (Brazzaville), violence continues to characterise the Pool region as government forces engage with rebel militias. In Congo (Kinshasa), warfare continues despite political progress towards a referendum and preparations for elections. War has resulted in over four million deaths in this blighted country since the start of the conflict on 2 August 1998. What is extremely worrisome is that fact that there has been a discernible spreading of the conflict from the Kivus in the East to other regions like Kasai and Katanga.

In Southern Africa, developments in four countries point to prospects of increasing conflict. As Angola goes to the polls, intimidation of opposition voters by the ruling party's Youth League is increasingly a source of concern. This intimidation might well provoke a backlash as the opposition increasingly responds with violence. In Swaziland, pro-democracy demonstrations against a feudal king have increasingly turned violent. In South Africa, frustration at poor service delivery—housing, water, electricity and sanitation—has resulted in violent demonstrations and attacks on local municipal councillors. At the time of this writing, large police contingents have entered the township of Khutsong to maintain some semblance of order. Meanwhile Zimbabwe remains poised on a knife-edge as the government confronts the opposition Movement for Democratic Change (MDC). A further challenge in Zimbabwe is that schisms have emerged inside both the ruling party and the opposition, complicating the search for peace.

The purpose of this brief overview of conflict in Africa is to point out an important truism—conflict persists in Africa despite advances on paper in Africa's security structure. These include the Peace and Security Council of the African Union (AU), an African Standby Force (ASF), a Council of the Wise to mediate disputes before they become violent and a Continental Early Warning System. Most observers are of the opinion that these structures will take some time before they can function independently and effectively. For instance, consider here the ASF, which lacks development of a common military doctrine, common command and control, common training, and a common logistics framework, not to mention adequate resources. It should also be noted here that the departure of the Nigerians and Rwandans who were to be deployed under the auspices of the AU to Darfur was delayed on account of the lack of a strategic airlift capability, which was eventually provided by the Americans. NATO was also called upon to assist the AU mission in Darfur, as it was lacking even basic communication equipment.

Given these limitations in Africa-based security, I strongly support the initiative of a UN Emergency Peace Service (UNEPS). As we continue to develop effective regional and international forces to protect the longer-term human security of Africa's long-suffering citizens, a UNEPS rapid reaction force could play a crucial role in stopping conflicts before they start or, at the very least, prevent their escalation. The time to act to prevent another Rwanda is now.

FORGING THE BASIS OF LEGITIMACY FOR UNEPS: SOUTH AMERICAN PERSPECTIVES

Alcides Costa Vaz

The need to provide the United Nations with an effective emergency peace service derives from the fact that genocide and mass violation of human rights—often associated with political grievances exacerbated by ethnical conflicts over territory or state control—remain a grave potential threat in several global regions. As the unfortunate record of the past decade shows, these are ineludible traces of contemporary reality; they have not faded despite all the political, economic and cultural changes the world has undergone. The difficulties of the international community at large and of the United Nations in particular to react promptly and effectively to imminent, grave humanitarian crises and the human, political and economic costs that follow them grant the UNEPS proposal a sense of urgency and opportunity and are, themselves, its foremost justification. Even considering that the risks of genocide and mass violations of human rights in the context of international and domestic conflicts are not equally present in all regions of the world, the preventive focus and humanitarian concerns which underlie the UNEPS proposal grants it a global appeal and a corresponding multilateral identity.

If the facts that make UNEPS a necessary and justifiable initiative are unquestionable, its political feasibility is not, as UNEPS raises and touches upon highly sensitive and differently valued political issues. For this reason, this is a proposal destined to encounter a wide range of concerns and reactions, in my opinion, from cautious criticism and resistance to overt objections lodged by the great powers, including the U.S., as well as those from intermediate powers and weak states. Actually, many of these concerns and objections have already been raised and are widely known, as the process through which UNEPS has been formulated has been both highly participatory and encompassing.

Therefore, the prospects for UNEPS to come into reality rely heavily on some key conditions which, in turn, reflect the very nature of the proposal. It is necessary, then, to focus on the most prominent features of the initiative in order to assess its political feasibility. UNEPS is intended to be primarily an *emergency*, *preventive* and *peace oriented* instrument at the disposal of the international community. Although conceived as a permanent standing instrument, UNEPS forces are designed to be deployed only in situations of imminent risk of genocide, of widespread violence and violation of human rights, or as a secondary resource to help populations severely threatened by natural disasters. UNEPS is also intended to be *complementary* and *non-exclusive* in relation to other existing multilateral and regional peace-making mechanisms. It is also *subsidiary* and thus subject to the political and operational control of existing UN bodies. It is essential that UNEPS be preserved from the discretionary interests of any single state or group of states. It will be thus *multilateral* as to its funding and to the provision of material and human resources, *multidimensional* as to its components and tasks, and *temporary* as to its own presence and activities. Once the emergency situation that led to initial UNEPS engagement is under control and other long lasting mechanisms for peace making have been established on the ground, UNEPS must give way to them.

These are the main defining characteristics that lie at the core of the UNEPS proposal. They must be taken into account when assessing its political feasibility since its legitimacy will derive not only from the humanitarian concerns it addresses but from the extent of support UNEPS will be granted from the international community at large. UNEPS will become a legitimate and reliable multilateral instrument as it shows itself decisively committed to its core priorities. In other words, it must be deprived of and insulated from any sort of casuistic interests or purposes that deviate from its fundamental aims. Some basic conditions must then be met to enhance prospects for UNEPS to achieve solid international endorsement and support:

(a) exhibiting a strong and exclusive commitment to the humanitarian concerns to which it is intended to respond;

(b) maintaining itself as a strictly and unambiguously principle-oriented initiative in its conception and its functioning;

(c) defining with clarity the criteria and procedures that will prevent UNEPS from being *captured* or misused by a particular country or group of countries.

These conditions do not suffice to deal with the full array of political and operational challenges that UNEPS might face. They are related only to the process of laying the groundwork for a sustained international legitimacy. In addition to these global confidence-building considerations, regionally focused approaches and concerns regarding this initiative are also necessary. In the following paragraphs an overall view of UNEPS prospects from the perspective of South America is presented.

South America is often regarded internationally as a stable region in relative terms when taking into account the occurrence or the prospects of inter-state conflict. Although the last war in the region was fought between Peru and Ecuador as recently as the mid-nineties, there are no immediate prospects of inter-state conflict in the region. Some territorial disputes still persist, but they have not been dealt with militarily. The great challenges to security at present arise from local violence mostly associated with the traffic of illegal drugs, arms and munitions, as well as the actions perpetrated by organized crime and urban gangs. Actually, due to the high levels of violence associated with criminality, South America is sometimes seen as one of the more insecure regions in the world. However, despite areas of high political and social instability—the lasting civil war in Colombia being the most acute example of a violence-driven process—political and social turmoil have not devolved into the internationalization of regional conflicts. At the same time, politically motivated violence has diminished significantly since the restoration of democracy in the mid-eighties.

South America as a region poses no real concerns regarding genocide. The human rights record of the region has gradually improved, even though several forms of violations associated with the repression of protests, the war on drugs, labor rights, migration, ethnic minorities and racial and sexual discrimination still persist in most of the countries in the region. South America is still exposed to political and social instability, high levels of local violence and human rights abuses, but not in an unmanageable or uncontrolled level as to require any form of international intervention. Thus, this would not likely become a focal region for UNEPS action. But, if the threats and challenges that UNEPS is expected to respond to are not impending crises in South America itself, this does not mean that the region should not devote attention and efforts to preventing abuse wherever it occurs. The human rights and humanitarian concerns to which UNEPS is designed to respond are universal, and South America should certainly embrace the challenges and responsibilities of promoting international stability and respect for human rights.

On the other hand, many South American countries express grave concerns regarding the specter of any form of interventionism, due to the history of unwelcome foreign involvements throughout Latin America. Being within the immediate sphere of influence of the United States and given perceptions of vulnerability in relation to their own political, economic and territorial sovereignty, intervention is an issue of extreme political sensitivity and relevance for many countries in the region. This concern has prevented most countries in the region from endorsing the principle of collective responsibility to protect and intervene in situations of grave human rights violations that lies at the core of the UNEPS proposal. Hence, it is necessary to clearly detach UNEPS from U.S. hegemony from the very beginning in order to assure South America that UNEPS is an instrument to prevent abuse and foster peace, not a program to threaten their sovereignty. Without this guarantee, countries like Brazil, Venezuela, Bolivia and Peru, to mention the most evident cases, will not be prone to endorse it.

Of course, there are positive incentives that can help win the support of the region for an emergency peace service. UNEPS is an initiative that can contribute to strengthening multilateralism and promoting international stability, objectives that rank high within the foreign policy agendas of all South American countries. UNEPS might also provide opportunities for the region to enhance its international profile in the realm of peacekeeping. Countries like Argentina, Brazil, Uruguay and Chile have actively engaged in peacekeeping operations sponsored by the United Nations on several occasions. UNEPS would provide an additional institutional space for that sort of engagement.

The main challenge at this point, however, is to address confidence-building measures in order to help South American governments view the UNEPS proposal in terms of what it must become: an emergency peace service to help the international community respond promptly to acute, immediate humanitarian crisis and not as an instrument of global power politics.

PREVENTING GENOCIDE: A UNITED NATIONS EMERGENCY PEACE SERVICE

Lois Barber

This is basic. The people and policymakers of the world can continue to be shocked, horrified, outraged and grief stricken by one genocide after another, or, we can take meaningful action to stop the killing.

Genocide doesn't just happen. The ideas and actions that lead to genocide come from the individual minds and collective will of human beings. The ideas and actions to *prevent* genocide will likewise come from our individual minds and collective will. Thankfully, a group of experienced and knowledgeable people from all regions of the world have been working together to develop a plan to relegate genocide to history—something we look back on with sorrow and regret. This group's plan for a United Nations Emergency Peace Service, UNEPS, is thoughtful, well researched and solid. When implemented, it will create a rapid, comprehensive, internationally legitimate response to acts of genocide and other crises and save millions of lives through preventive action.

The United Nations, as we know it, has serious limitations that prevent it from taking the necessary quick action in response to a crisis like genocide. However, there is now growing international support to remove those limitations and give the UN the authority and capacity needed to make a rapid response to emergency situations characterized by gross violations of human rights.

In 1998, EarthAction, the world's largest network of organizations that take action together for a more just, peaceful and sustainable world, surveyed its then 1,434 Partner Organizations in over 150 countries about their support for a UN rapid response emergency service.

More than 570 organizations responded to the survey. Of those, 94 percent supported the creation of a UN rapid deployment service that could respond immediately to genocidal aggression in order to protect innocent lives. I am certain that in 2006, an even greater percentage of EarthAction's now 2,200 Partner Organizations would agree that the world needs a UN rapid response to fast-breaking human rights crises.

In 2000, EarthAction commissioned a poll of a representative sample of U.S. voters to learn their views on critical foreign policy issues. Sixty-five percent of those polled supported the creation of a permanent UN force made up of individual volunteers ready to be sent quickly to conflict areas to stop violence and prevent mass murder. We were so encouraged by this response that we ran full page ads in the *New York Times* and other papers throughout the United States to publicize these poll results, believing that when the people lead the leaders will follow.

They aren't following quite yet. The world's national governments now have more than 40 million men and women in military uniform. Yet, as genocide commences and spreads, the global community continues to be completely unequipped to respond. It remains clear that we need a UN protection service of highly trained and highly motivated volunteers, ready to take whatever risks are necessary to prevent the murder of innocent people.

To be fully effective, a UN Emergency Peace Service needs to be combined with other steps to strengthen the peacemaking and peacekeeping capacities of the United Nations. No matter what other steps are taken, though, without a standing volunteer force the UN will have no effective way to confront aggression and massive abuses of human rights. Until such a force is created, we are all too likely to watch in horror yet again, as innocents are murdered—waiting for help that never arrives.

The plan to create UNEPS offers a way forward. Let us build support for it at every level and in every nation, and create the political will to make it a reality.

APPENDIX A:
CALL FOR ENDORSEMENTS AND COMMENTS

The Working Group for a United Nations Emergency Peace Service is seeking endorsements for this proposal as well as constructive comment and criticism from non-governmental organizations, international civil servants at the United Nations and regional organizations, scholars, government officials, and other interested persons. Communications about this proposal should be sent to Global Action to Prevent War at this e-mail address: coordinator@globalactionpw.org with a copy to the rapporteur at Johansen.2@nd.edu. The home page URL is www.globalactionpw.org.

Secretariat functions are being shared by Global Action to Prevent War, the Nuclear Age Peace Foundation, and the World Federalist Movement.

If you individually or your organization endorse this proposal in principle, particularly as described in the Executive Summary in Chapter 1, please inform us at the preceding email addresses or write to us at:

> The UNEPS Initiative
> c/o Global Action to Prevent War
> 675 Third Avenue, Suite 315
> New York, NY 10017
> United States of America

APPENDIX B:
CONFERENCE PARTICIPANTS

The following were participants at the symposium on "Genocide and Crimes Against Humanity: The Challenge of Prevention and Enforcement," co-sponsored by the Nuclear Age Peace Foundation; the Simons Centre for Peace and Disarmament Studies, Liu Institute for Global Issues, University of British Columbia; Global Action to Prevent War; and the Law and Society Program, University of California, Santa Barbara, December 5-6, 2003.

Lloyd Axworthy, Former Canadian Foreign Minister; President, University of Winnipeg

Manou Eskandari-Qajar, Professor of Political Science, Santa Barbara City College

Richard Falk, Professor Emeritus of International Law, Princeton University; Chair, Nuclear Age Peace Foundation

Lisa Hajjar, Professor, Law and Society Program, University of California Santa Barbara

Peter Haslund, Director of the International and Global Studies Program, Santa Barbara City College

Robert C. Johansen, Senior Fellow, Kroc Institute for International Peace Studies and Professor of Political Science, University of Notre Dame

Don Kraus, Executive Vice President, Citizens for Global Solutions

David Krieger, President, Nuclear Age Peace Foundation

H. Peter Langille, University of Western Ontario; Director, Global Human Security: Ideas & Initiatives

Saul Mendlovitz, Dag Hammarskjøld Professor of International Law, Rutgers Law School; Co-director, World Order Models Project; Co-founder Global Action to Prevent War

William Pace, Executive Director, World Federalist Movement; Convener, International Coalition for the International Criminal Court

James Paul, Executive Director, Global Policy Forum

Jennifer Allen Simons, President, The Simons Foundation; Adjunct and Associate Professor, Institute for the Humanities, Simon Fraser University

Alice Slater, President, Global Resource Action Center for the Environment; Founder, Abolition 2000

Joanna Weschler, Director of Research, Security Council Report

The following were participants at the United Nations Emergency Peace Service conference co-hosted by Global Action to Prevent War, the Center for Peace Research in Madrid, and the faculty of social sciences at the University of Castilla–La Mancha. The meeting was made possible by a grant from the Ford Foundation and financial support from the Global Legal Studies Program of Rutgers University School of Law.

Mariano Aguirre, Co-director and Coordinator, Peace and Security and Human Rights programmes, La Fundación para las Relaciones Internacionales y el Diálogo Exterior

Lois Barber, Executive Director, EarthAction North America; Creative Director, the World Future Council Initiative

Jörg Calließ, Director of Studies, Evangelische Akademie Loccum

Kevin Clements, Professor and Director, the Australian Centre for Peace and Conflict Studies, The University of Queensland

Alcides Costa Vaz, Professor of International Relations and Executive Coordinator, Center for Mercosur Studies, Instituto de Relações Internacionais, Universidade de Brasília

Merav Datan, Adjunct Professor, Rutgers Law School; Board Member, The Lawyers' Committee on Nuclear Policy

Jonathan Dean, Former United States Ambassador; Adviser on Security Issues, Union of Concerned Scientists

Mabel González Bustelo, Researcher, Centro de Investigación para la Paz

Jose Luis Herrero, Director, Fundación para las Relaciones, Internacionales y el Diálogo Exterior

Felicity Hill, Medical Association for Prevention of War, Australian affiliate of International Physicians for the Prevention of Nuclear War

Robert C. Johansen, Senior Fellow, Kroc Institute for International Peace Studies and Professor of Political Science, University of Notre Dame

Rebecca Johnson, Executive Director, The Acronym Institute for Disarmament Diplomacy

Don Kraus, Executive Vice President, Citizens for Global Solutions

H. Peter Langille, University of Western Ontario; Director, Global Human Security: Ideas & Initiatives

Sarah Martin, Advocate, Refugees International

Juan Mendez, Special Adviser to the United Nations Secretary-General on the Prevention of Genocide; President, International Center for Transitional Justice

Saul Mendlovitz, Dag Hammarskjøld Professor of International Law, Rutgers Law School; Co-director, World Order Models Project; Co-founder Global Action to Prevent War

Manuela Mesa, Director, Centro de Investigación para la Paz

Bjørn Møller, Senior Researcher, Danish Institute for International Studies

Radmila Nakarada, Senior Researcher, President of Scientific Council, and Executive Board Member of the Institute for European Studies

Satish Nambiar, Lt. Gen. (retired) Indian Army, and former Commander of UN forces in the former Yugoslavia; Director, The United Service Institution of India

Ricardo Navarro, Chairman, Friends of the Earth International

Jennifer Nordstrom, Project Associate, Women's International League for Peace and Freedom; former Coordinator, Global Action to Prevent War

Juan Miguel Ortega Terol, Professor of International Public Law, Facultad de Ciencias Sociales, Universidad de Castilla-La Mancha

William Pace, Executive Director, World Federalist Movement; Convener, International Coalition for the International Criminal Court

Stuart Rees, Professor Emeritus, Center for Peace and Conflict Studies, University of Sydney

Waheguru Pal Singh Sidhu, Faculty, the Geneva Center for Security Policy

Hussein Solomon, Professor and Director, Centre for International Political Studies, University of Pretoria

Alejandro Soto Romero, Coordinator, Epidemiology Surveillance, Emergencies and Disasters, Ministry of Health, Mexico

Sharon Welch, Professor and Director of Graduate Studies, Department of Religious Studies, University of Missouri-Columbia

Joanna Weschler, Director of Research, Security Council Report

Bo Wirmark, Former Chairman, Swedish Peace Council

Detlev Wolter, Head of Division, EU Policy and Law, State Chancellery Brandenburg, Germany

Xavier Zeebroek, Research Fellow, Groupe de Recherche et de l'Information sur la Paix et la Sécurité

Wei Zonglei, Research Fellow and Deputy Director, Center for US-Europe Studies, China Institutes of Contemporary International Relations

Nieves Zuñiga, Researcher, Centro de Investigación para la Paz

FOR FURTHER READING

Campbell, Kenneth J. *Genocide and the Global Village*. Basingstoke: Palgrave, 2001.

Canada, Government of. *Towards a Rapid Reaction Capability for the United Nations*. Ottawa: Government of Canada, 1995.

Bloomfield, Lincoln P., ed. *International Military Forces: The Question of Peacekeeping in an Armed and Disarming World*. Boston: Little, Brown, 1964.

Bowett, D. W. *United Nations Forces: A Legal Study*. New York: Praeger, 1964.

Clark, Grenville and Louis Sohn. *World Peace Through World Law: Two Alternative Plans*. Cambridge: Harvard University Press, 1966.

Danish Ministry of Foreign Affairs. *Background Paper About Establishing a Multinational U.N. Standby Forces Brigade at High Readiness (Shirbrig)*. Copenhagen: Government of Denmark, 1996.

Fetherston, A.B. *Towards a Theory of United Nations Peacekeeping*. Basingstoke: St. Martin's, 1994.

Heidenrich, John G. *How to Prevent Genocide: A Guide for Policymakers, Scholars and the Concerned Citizen*. Westport, CN: Praeger, 2001.

International Commission on Intervention and State Sovereignty. *The Responsibility to Protect*. Ottawa: International Development Research Centre, 2001.

Johansen, Robert C. "The Future of United Nations Peacekeeping and Enforcement: A Framework for Policymaking." *Global Governance 2*, no. 3 (1996): 299-333.

Kaldor, Mary. *New and Old Wars: Organised Violence in a Global Era*. Cambridge: Polity Press, 2001.

Kinloch, Stephen P. "Utopian or Pragmatic? A U.N. Permanent Military Volunteer Force." *International Peacekeeping 3*, no. 4 (1996): 166-90.

Langille, H. Peter. *Bridging the Commitment-Capacity Gap: A Review of Existing Arrangements and Options for Enhancing U.N. Rapid Deployment*. Wayne, NJ: Center for U.N. Reform Education, 2002.

Leurdijk, Dick A. "Rapid Deployment: The Capacity Gap." In *A UN Rapid Deployment Brigade: Strengthening the Capacity for Quick Response*. The Hague: Netherlands Institute of International Relations, 1995.

Mendlovitz, Saul, and John Fousek. "A U.N. Constabulary to Enforce the Law on Genocide and Crimes against Humanity." In *Protection against Genocide: Mission Impossible?* edited by Neal Riemer. Westport: Praeger, 2000: 105-122.

Morgenthau, Hans. "Political Conditions for a Force." In *International Military Forces,* edited by Lincoln P. Bloomfield. Boston: Little, Brown, 1964: 175-186.

Netherlands, Government of the. *The Netherlands Non-Paper: A U.N. Rapid Deployment Brigade: A Preliminary Study*. The Hague: Government of the Netherlands, 1995.

Power, Samantha. *A Problem from Hell: America and the Age of Genocide*. New York: Basic Books, 2002.

Riemer, Neal, ed. *Protection against Genocide: Mission Impossible?* Westport: Praeger, 2000.

Roberts, Adam. "Proposals for U.N. Standing Forces: History, Tasks and Obstacles." In *U.N. Rapid Reaction Capabilities: Requirements and Prospects*, edited by David Cox and Albert Legault. Cornwallis: The Canadian Peacekeeping Press, 1995.

Standby High Readiness Brigade for United Nations Operations. 2006. *Memorandum of Understanding Concerning Operation, Funding, Administration and Status of the Multinational United Nations Stand-by Forces High Readiness Brigade.* Available at http://www.shirbrig.dk/shirbrig/documents/MOU%20SB.pdf.

United Nations. *Report of the Panel on United Nations Peace Operations*, A/55/305-S/2000/809. New York: United Nations, 2000.

United Nations Special Committee on Peacekeeping. *Under-Secretary-General for Peacekeeping Operations Tells Special Committee Operations Must Deploy Credibility, Rapidly to Succeed,* GA/PK/174. New York: United Nations, 2002.

United Nations High-level Panel on Threats, Challenges, and Change. *A More Secure World: Our Shared Responsibility*, A/59/565. New York: United Nations, 2004.

Urquhart, Brian. "For a U.N. Volunteer Military Force." *New York Review of Books,* 10 June 1993:3-4.

———. "Prospects for UN Rapid Response Capability." In *U.N. Rapid Reaction Capabilities: Requirements and Prospects,* edited by David Cox and Albert Legault. Cornwallis: The Canadian Peacekeeping Press, 1995: 3-35.

CONTRIBUTORS

Lois Jewel Barber is Co-creator and Executive Director of EarthAction, an international network of over 2,200 citizen's groups in 163 countries that have worked together on 83 campaigns focused on global environment, development, peace, and human rights issues. She is also Creative Director of the World Future Council Initiative. She founded and serves as the President of 20/20 Vision, a U.S. peace and environment organization. She lectures widely and has received many awards including the "Woman of Distinction Award" by the National Women's Education Association and was one of 16 global citizens featured in the book, *Planet Champions—Adventures in Saving the World.*

Alcides Costa Vaz is the Director of the Institute of International Relations of the University of Brasilia, Brazil. He holds a Ph.D. degree in social science and the sociology of international relations, University of Sao Paulo, and an M.A. degree in international relations. He is the author of many books and articles on international security, regional politics and integration, and Brazilian foreign policy. His current research focuses on the role of emerging powers in international security and regional security cooperation in South America.

Robert C. Johansen is Senior Fellow at the Kroc Institute for International Peace Studies and Professor of Political Science at the University of Notre Dame. He is author of *The National Interest and the Human Interest: An Analysis of U.S. Foreign Policy* (Princeton University Press) and numerous articles on normative international relations, the United Nations, and global governance. He has held visiting research appointments at Princeton and Harvard. His current research focuses on efforts to increase compliance with the prohibitions of war crimes, genocide, crimes against humanity, and crimes against the peace.

David Krieger is a founder of the Nuclear Age Peace Foundation, and has served as President of the Foundation since 1982. He has lectured through-out the United States, Europe, and Asia on issues of peace, security, international law, and the abolition of nuclear weapons. He serves as an adviser to many peace organizations around the world and has received many awards for his work for a more peaceful and nuclear weapons-free world. Author of numerous studies of peace in the Nuclear Age, his most recent books are *Hold Hope, Wage Peace*; *Einstein—Peace Now!*; *Today Is Not a Good Day for War* (Poetry); *Peace 100 Ideas*; *Hope in a Dark Time, Reflections on Humanity's Future*; *The Poetry of Peace*; and *Choose Hope, Your Role in Waging Peace in the Nuclear Age*.

Saul Mendlovitz is Dag Hammarskjold Professor of Peace and World Order Studies, Rutgers School of Law. He held the Ira D. Wallach Professor of World Order Studies at Columbia University School of International Affairs (1979-87) and was visiting Professor of Law, University of Chicago Law School. He has written and spoken extensively on international law and the promotion of a just world order. He has published and edited ten volumes on these matters, including: *A Reader on Second Assembly and Parliamentary Proposals* (edited with Barbara Walker); *Preferred Futures for the United Nations*; and *A U.N. Constabulary to Enforce the Law on Genocide and Crimes Against Humanity* with John Fousek. Professor Mendlovitz is the founding director of the World Order Models Project and a founding member of Global Action to Prevent War. He represents four organizations at the United Nations: The International Association of Lawyers Against Nuclear Arms, The Lawyers Committee on Nuclear Policy, The International Peace Research Association, and The World Future Studies Federation.

Satish Nambiar is a Lieutenant General in the Indian Army, PVSM, AVSM, VRC (retired). He served in Jammu and Kashmir, counter insurgency operations in the North East, and active participation in the 1965 and 1971 operations in the Indian sub-continent. A graduate of the Australian Staff College, he was on the faculty of the Defence Services Staff College, and served as Military Adviser at the High Commission of India in London. As Director General of Military Operations in 1991, he led two delegations for talks with Pakistan. He was Head of the United Nations forces in the former Yugoslavia. From 2003-2004 he served on the 16 member High Level Panel appointed by the United Nations Secretary-General on Threats, Challenges and Change. Lt. Gen. Satish Nambiar is currently the Director of the United Service Institution of India.

William R. Pace has served as the Executive Director of the World Federalist Movement-Institute for Global Policy, a 59-year old peace movement dedicated to promoting international democracy, global justice, and the rule of law, since 1994. In 1995, Mr. Pace was asked to serve as the Convenor of the NGO Coalition for an International Criminal Court, an international network which has grown since that time to comprise more than 2,000 organizations. Mr. Pace served as the Secretary-General for the Hague Appeal for Peace civil society conference in 1999, a monumental gathering for peace in the city of The Hague in the Netherlands. From 2002 through 2004, Mr. Pace also served as the President of the Center for United Nations Reform Education. Mr. Pace is a co-founder of numerous NGO networks and steering committees, including the NGO Steering Committee for the UN Commission on Sustainable Development; the Washington Coalition for Human Rights; and the International NGO Task Group on Legal and Institutional Matters.

Hussein Solomon is Professor and Director of the Centre for International Political Studies. He lectures in the Department of Political Science at the University of Pretoria, South Africa. He speaks and writes extensively on African international relations and security issues. He is also an Executive Committee Member of Global Action to Prevent War. His research interests include conflict resolution, multilateral security institutions, and religious fundamentalism. His most recent publication is entitled *Exploring Islamic Fundamentalist Ideologies in Africa* published by the Africa Institute (Pretoria, South Africa, 2006).

Brian Urquhart was one of the first United Nations civil servants. He joined the UN Secretariat in 1945 after six years of war service in the British Army. He served as personal assistant to the first Secretary-General, Trygve Lie, and subsequently worked closely with five Secretaries-General on peace and security matters, especially peacekeeping. He was Under Secretary-General for Special Political Affairs from 1972 to 1986, when he retired. For the next ten years he was scholar-in-residence in the international affairs program at the Ford Foundation. His books include, *A Life in Peace and War,* a memoir, *Hammarskjold,* a biography of the second Secretary-General, *Decolonization and World Peace,* and *Ralph Bunche: An American Odyssey.*

SPONSORING ORGANIZATIONS

Global Action to Prevent War

Global Action to Prevent War (GAPW) is an emerging transnational network dedicated to practical measures for reducing global levels of conflict and to removing the institutional and ideological impediments to ending armed violence and severe human rights violations. GAPW grounds the goal of conflict prevention in specific integrated phases over a three to four-decade period, and demonstrates in a concrete way that we can move from an international system based on conflict and power relations to one based on law and multilateral institutions. This reasonable timetable integrates action towards successive advances in early warning, prevention of armed conflict, nonviolent means of conflict resolution, peacekeeping and peacemaking, transparency and other confidence-building measures, disarmament, and the implementation of criminal law regarding genocide and crimes against humanity.

www.globalactionpw.org

Nuclear Age Peace Foundation

The Nuclear Age Peace Foundation initiates and supports worldwide efforts to abolish nuclear weapons, to strengthen international law and institutions, and to empower a new generation of peace leaders. Founded in 1982, the Foundation is comprised of individuals and organizations worldwide who realize the imperative for peace in the Nuclear Age. It is a non-profit, non-partisan international education and advocacy organization with consultative status to the United Nations Economic and Social Council. The Foundation is recognized as a United Nations Peace Messenger organization. In December 2003, the Foundation hosted an International Law Symposium on "Genocide and Crimes against Humanity: The Challenge of Prevention and Enforcement," which brought together a group of expert participants to explore the need to create a United Nations Emergency Peace Service.

www.wagingpeace.org

World Federalist Movement

The World Federalist Movement (WFM) is an international non-governmental organization working to promote democratic global governance and international democracy. The World Federalist Movement-Institute for Global Policy has been dedicated to deep and democratic reform of the United Nations for more than five decades. WFM-IGP seeks to promote the application of the federalist constitutional political philosophy, including the principle of subsidiarity, to international governance. WFM is a membership and citizen's movement working for justice, peace, and sustainable prosperity. We call for an end to the rule of force, through a world governed by law, based on strengthened and democratized world institutions. World federalists support the creation of democratic global structures accountable to the citizens of the world and call for the division of international authority among separate agencies. WFM has helped found and lead CURE, the Coalition for the International Criminal Court, the Hague Appeal for Peace, the Responsibility to Protect – Engaging Civil Society Network, ReformtheUN.org and numerous other international networks and campaigns.

www.wfm.org